AN EYE SINGLE TO
THE GLORY OF GOD

AN EYE SINGLE TO THE GLORY OF GOD

Reflections on the Cost of Discipleship

Robert L. Millet

Deseret Book Company
Salt Lake City, Utah

Library of Congress Cataloging-in-Publication Data

Millet, Robert L.
    An eye single to the glory of God : reflections on the cost of discipleship / Robert L. Millet.
        p.   cm.
    Includes bibliographical references and index.
    ISBN 0-87579-392-4
    1. Christian life—Mormon authors.   I. Title.
BX8656.M54 1991
248.4′89332—dc20   90-48800
                                                                         CIP

Printed in the United States of America

10   9   8   7   6   5   4   3   2   1

CONTENTS

CONTENTS

THE FRUITS OF DISCIPLESHIP

PREFACE

Some twenty-five years ago I sat in the home of a friend a few hours before I was to leave Salt Lake City for a mission to the eastern United States. This friend's powerful missionary example had helped me decide to serve a mission. "Gary," I asked, "what could you say to help me be a successful missionary?"

He didn't even hesitate: "You keep an eye single to the glory of God, and you'll be successful." I thanked him for his counsel, but inwardly I felt cheated. Surely, I thought, there was something more specific that could make me a better finder, teacher, and baptizer.

I was in the mission field only two days before the import of his advice started to become evident. He could not have hit the mark more directly. Over the years since, I have discovered how vital this principle is in the work of the kingdom. The task of the disciple of Christ is to deny self, to seek the way of the Master, to be willing to forsake the manmade and the material, and to pursue with steadfastness the divine and the everlasting. For the disciple, it is the kingdom of God, or nothing. I confess that I have not always been true to this principle, but whenever I have, the power and goodness of God have flowed freely.

The brief chapters in this book about discipleship focus directly on some phase of that sacred enterprise — the call, the costs, and the fruits of discipleship. In a day when people are encouraged from all sides to "do their own thing" or to "march to a different drum," Christ invites his people to come unto him, partake of his goodness and grace, acquire his nature, and seek to obtain his mind. The irony of such complete surrender and submission is in that the true disciple is thereby put on the path that leads to absolute freedom and true self-fulfillment.

Because knowledge and understanding are cumulative, it is not always possible to identify and express specific appreciation to all those who have helped along the way. In the preparation of this manuscript—from outline and ideas to paragraphs and chapters—I owe a special debt of gratitude to Joell Woodbrey, a dear friend as well as a conscientious secretary and assistant, who has enthusiastically read each chapter and offered helpful suggestions. I thank Ron Millett, president of Deseret Book Company, for encouraging me in this project, as well as Suzanne Brady, editor, for her assistance along the way to finished product. For what follows in this volume I am indebted to friends and colleagues and teachers and Church leaders—many of whom have exemplified the principles which will be discussed herein—but I alone am responsible for the conclusions drawn from the evidence cited. This book is a private endeavor and not an official publication of either The Church of Jesus Christ of Latter-day Saints or of Brigham Young University.

To walk as a disciple is to walk in the light, to forsake darkness, to cleave unto him who is the Light. To be a disciple is to seek to be changed, to open oneself to the transforming powers of Jesus the Christ. "And if your eye be single to my glory," the Lord has explained, "your whole bodies shall be filled with light, and there shall be no darkness in you; and that body which is filled with light comprehendeth all things." To become a disciple of Christ is to enter the realm of divine experience and thereby begin to see and feel things as the Master does. The disciple, the agent of the Lord, seeks in process of time to be like his Principal and eventually to be worthy of being with Him. "Therefore, sanctify yourselves *that your minds become single to God,* and the days will come that you shall see him; for he will unveil his face unto you, and it shall be in his own time, and in his own way, and according to his own will" (D&C 88:67–68; emphasis added).

Such is the cost and the task of the follower of Jesus Christ. And such is the transcendent privilege that comes through a life of dedicated discipleship.

THE CALL TO DISCIPLESHIP

Chapter 1

YE ARE MY DISCIPLES

Jesus Christ calls us to his service. He bids us to follow him, to walk in his steps. Our Lord seeks to make of us *disciples*.

"Come, follow me" was and is the Savior's simple invitation to forsake the world, discard the irrelevant, and cling to that which is of lasting worth. It is an invitation to join him, to enjoy fellowship with him and his, and to eventually receive the promised reward of the disciple. The Master's plea is everlastingly the same: "Come unto me all ye ends of the earth, buy milk and honey, without money and without price" (2 Ne. 26:25; Isa. 55:1). Association with the Holy One is a prize which is freely bestowed. It may not be purchased with money nor bartered for in the marketplaces of the world. It is a gift, a priceless treasure granted by him to whom all things humbly bow. And yet it is to be bought with a price, a heavy price. Though we may not acquire its benefits through exchanging gold and silver, it costs us everything. Our hearts. Our lives. Herein is a victory that is achieved only through unconditional surrender.

Jehovah pronounced a scathing denunciation upon most of mankind: "My people have committed two evils; they have forsaken me the fountain of living waters, and hewed them out cisterns, broken cisterns, that can hold no water" (Jer. 2:13). All people thirst for the living waters, even those who do not know they do. And, unfortunately, many spend endless hours and needed strength in digging their own wells or searching for water when the cooling draught of the Redeemer is within easy reach.

3

Jesus Christ offers deliverance from the superficial and the shallow. He offers a saving alternative to programs which are woefully deficient or even plainly perverse. His way, the gospel way, is easy to those who pursue it with singlemindedness. It is more difficult for those who embark on the Christian cause with hesitation or reservation. Those who have charted their course and pointed themselves toward the abundant life in Christ have their challenges, their difficulties, like anyone else. They meet these roadblocks, however, with courage and perspective, with a quiet confidence borne of the Spirit. Such individuals have no difficulty living the gospel. It is not hard. It is not burdensome. For disciples of Christ, living the gospel is a lifting and liberating experience. In the ultimate sense, President Brigham Young explained, "the man or woman who enjoys the spirit of our religion has no trials; but the man or woman who tries to live according to the Gospel of the Son of God, and at the same time clings to the spirit of the world, has trials and sorrows acute and keen, and that, too, continually.

"This is the deciding point, the dividing line. They who love and serve God with all their hearts rejoice evermore, pray without ceasing, and in everything give thanks; but they who try to serve God and still cling to the spirit of the world, have got on two yokes—the yoke of Jesus and the yoke of the devil, and they will have plenty to do. They will have a warfare inside and outside, and the labor will be very galling, for they are directly in opposition one to the other. Cast off the yoke of the enemy, and put on the yoke of Christ, and you will say that his yoke is easy and his burden is light. This I know by experience."[1]

This is not to say that discipleship is a bed of roses. We shall certainly have our share of heartache. There will undoubtedly be moments of discouragement and seasons of loneliness. But disciples of Christ are in this for life. We live by covenant: the terms of the covenant are stipulated by our Principal, and we as agents agree to abide by them. Those who seem to feel the greatest anxiety, the deepest frustration, are those who want to take charge, to set or reset the terms of the contract, who have a better idea. In short, those persons who demand their independence, who scream the loudest, "I can handle it!" who insist on being the master of their fate—these are they who never know the quiet but steady empowerment that comes from trusting in the infinite goodness of a Greater.

Disciples are those who have disciplined themselves, who have chosen to be pupils or followers, who have agreed to be taught or trained by another. Disciples are those who have committed themselves to a course, dedicated themselves to a cause. Disciples of Christ are those who have gained the witness that the path laid out by Jesus of Nazareth is the only and true path to peace and fulfillment here and eternal life hereafter. True disciples seek not alone to imitate the deeds and actions of their Lord but also to acquire Christian attributes—to draw upon those cleansing and renovating powers of His Spirit, which transform and convert. Disciples seek the divine nature of Christ. Christian discipleship entails more than hero worship. It consists of far more than admiring a Samaritan Socrates, more than finding fascination with a Galilean Guru. Jesus Christ is the Lord Omnipotent. He was and is God. Thus "Christianity without the living Christ is inevitably Christianity without discipleship, and Christianity without discipleship is always Christianity without Christ."[2] We see then that Christian discipleship transcends adherence to an idea, even devotion to an ideal. The power unto life and salvation is in Christ, the Person. The road of discipleship does not end in merely being *with* the Master, as sublime as such a reunion will be; discipleship results in being even as he is, for "when he shall appear, we shall be like him; for we shall see him as he is" (1 Jn. 3:2; Moro. 7:48).

In the end we shall surely see that the depth of our discipleship is to be gauged as much by our hearts and our desires as by the outward performance of our duties. Indeed, though some things may be ascertained only by physical evidence, some other things are hidden from the natural eye: they are known only to God. A man's heartfelt resolve to serve God at all hazards, a woman's inspired determination to do things the Lord's way, a couple's joint decision to seek first the kingdom of God—these are silent statements of the soul. They represent personal commitments to the Almighty. And one day the Eternal Father, who sees and hears in secret, shall reward such persons openly and abundantly.

NOTES

1. *Journal of Discourses,* 26 vols. (Liverpool: F. D. Richards, 1851–86), 16:123.
2. Dietrich Bonhoeffer, *The Cost of Discipleship,* rev. ed. (New York: Macmillan, 1963), pp. 63–64.

Chapter 2

HOW LONG HALT YE
BETWEEN TWO OPINIONS?

The Lord, in speaking with apocalyptic finality, said: "There are save two churches only; the one is the church of the Lamb of God, and the other is the church of the devil; wherefore, whoso belongeth not to the church of the Lamb of God belongeth to that great church, which is the mother of abominations; and she is the whore of all the earth" (1 Ne. 14:10). From the eternal perspective, from where God stands, there is only the course charted by him and advocated by the Savior and his prophets. Whatsoever is more or less than the divinely established plan is either deficient or perverse. No matter the degree of sincerity, adherence to anything less than the truth leads ultimately to a diluted discipleship.

"No man can serve two masters," said the Master, "for either he will hate the one, and love the other; or else he will hold to the one, and despise the other. Ye cannot serve God and mammon" (Matt. 6:24). Holding back or giving less than is required always produces divided loyalties. We need not have our membership records in the great and abominable church in order to be disloyal to the kingdom of God; the issue is not where our records are but rather where our hearts are. The divine word is certain: "there are many called, but few are chosen," because their hearts are set upon the things of this world, rather than upon those things which have eternal worth (D&C 121:34–35).

James explained that "a double minded man is unstable in all his ways" (James 1:8). The instability comes much less from lack of native strength than from lack of concentration and focus. Whatever receives from us less than our best will bring forth less than the best results and less than the best reward. Joseph Smith thus taught that a religion that does not require the sacrifice of all things never has the power to produce the faith necessary unto life and salvation.[1] Those who refuse to give their all to the Lord, whether by public declaration or by private volition, cannot enjoy the peace and power of single-minded obedience. Cain and his followers "loved Satan more than God" (Moses 5:13, 18, 28). It is not necessarily true that they did not love God. They may have. They simply loved Satan more! Their lives were centered upon Lucifer's enticements, upon his values, upon his rewards. Such a thing might not even be uncommon in our own day. Whenever we reserve our religion for one day in a week, we come awfully close to loving the things of a fallen world more than we love the things of the world to come.

The Lord counseled us in the Sermon on the Mount: "Enter ye in at the strait gate: for wide is the gate, and broad is the way, that leadeth to destruction, and many there be which go in thereat" (Matt. 7:13). That is, "the broad way is certainly easier. There is no precipice. There is plenty of latitude for those who want to sample the moral smorgasbord offered by the crowd on this road. There are hardly any limitations, no curbs, no boundaries. There is tolerance of every conceivable sin—just as long as you say you love Jesus. Or as long as you're religious or whatever else you want to be"[2] On the other hand, "strait is the gate, and narrow is the way, which leadeth unto life, and few there be that find it" (Matt. 7:14). The way is not impossible, only narrow. "In fact, many commentators would say that the best contemporary expression of the narrow gate is a turnstile. Only one person can pass through at a time"[3]

So often the prophets and seers—those who perceive things not visible to the natural eye (Moses 6:36)—are able to tear away the cobwebs of social sophistication and relativity and testify of the simple choice required of disciples of Christ. They sense that it is one way or the other. Moses demanded of Israel an answer to the eternal query: "Who is on the Lord's side?" (Ex. 32:26). Joshua likewise sounded a cry that signaled a time of decision: "Now therefore fear the Lord, and serve him in sincerity and in truth: and put away the gods which your fathers served on the other side of the flood, and in Egypt; and serve ye the Lord. And if it seem evil unto you to serve the Lord, choose you this day whom ye will serve; . . . but as for me and my house, we will serve the Lord" (Josh. 24:14–15; compare Moses 6:33). Elijah the Tishbite asked of a people who were easily wafted about by false gods: "How long halt ye between two opinions?" Then he commanded: "If the Lord be God, follow him" (1 Kgs. 18:21).

Our hearts cannot be wedded to another endeavor. Our might or strength cannot be spent in secondary causes. Our minds cannot be committed to another enterprise. In the words of the early brethren of this dispensation, it must be the kingdom of God or nothing. Those who fail to place the Savior at the center of their lives rob all other vital relationships of the potency that might otherwise be possible. Individuals who are unduly committed to work or hobby, for example, rather than to Christ and his kingdom, cannot enjoy the sweet fruits of gospel living; nor can their spouses and children and other associates participate in that elevating influence which comes from God. "I know thy works," the Lord warned the Laodiceans, "that thou art neither cold nor hot: I would thou wert cold or hot. So then because thou art lukewarm, and neither cold nor hot, I will spue [vomit] thee out of my mouth" (Rev. 3:15–16). People who are divided in their loyalties are prone to be half-hearted in their obedience. "There neither are nor can be any neutrals in this war," Elder Bruce R. McConkie taught. "Every member of the Church is on one side or the other. . . . In this war all who do not stand forth courageously and valiantly are by that fact alone aiding the cause of the enemy. 'They who are not for me are against me, saith our God.' (2 Ne. 10:16). We are either for the Church or we are against it. We either take its part or we take the consequences. We cannot survive spiritually with one foot in the Church and the other in the world. We must make the choice. It is either the Church or the world. There is no middle ground."[4]

The Light of Christ is given to every person who is born into the world. This moral monitor is the source of reason and conscience, a fundamental light that can direct our lives and prepare us for a greater revelation. In the words of the prophet-editor Mormon, this light or Spirit "is given unto you to judge, that ye may know good from evil; and the way to judge is as plain, that ye may know with a perfect knowledge, as the daylight is from the dark night. For behold," he continues, "the Spirit of Christ is given to every man, that he may know good from evil" (Moro. 7:15–16). In particular, baptized members of the Church need not be confused or deceived in regard to the ways of the world and the ways of God, for "by the power of the Holy Ghost [we] may know the truth of all things" (Moro. 10:5). There need be few, if any, gray areas in the struggle between good and evil; our spiritual sensitivity to right and wrong, pertinent and irrelevant, can be refined and heightened if we hearken consistently to our consciences. By so doing, we are able to discern clearly where the Lord stands on all matters of substance.

"There are two influences in the world today," said President George Albert Smith, "and have been from the beginning. One is an influence that is constructive, that radiates happiness and builds character. The other influence is one that destroys, turns men into demons, tears down and discourages. We are all susceptible to both.

"My grandfather used to say to his family, 'There is a line of demarkation, well defined, between the Lord's territory and the devil's. If you will stay on the Lord's side of the line you will be under his influence and will have no desire to do wrong; but if you cross to the devil's side of the line one inch, you are in the tempter's power, and if he is successful, you will not be able to think or even reason properly, because you will have lost the Spirit of the Lord.'

"When I have been tempted sometimes to do a certain thing, I have asked myself, "Which side of the line am I on?' If I determined to be on the safe side, the Lord's side, I would do the right thing every time. So when temptation comes, think prayerfully about your problem, and the influence of the Spirit of the Lord will enable you to decide wisely. There is safety for us only on the Lord's side of the line.

"If you want to be happy," President Smith concluded, "remember, that all happiness worthy of the name is on the Lord's side of the line and all sorrow and disappointment is on the devil's side of the line." [5]

It is comforting to know that we need not become holy in a day. Our quest for sainthood is gradual, and the climb is steep. Enoch's Zion was established "in process of time" (Moses 7:21), and with but few exceptions, the pure in heart become so in the same manner. Nor need we traverse the stony path to perfection alone. Indeed, we cannot. C. S. Lewis has observed that in a marvelous manner "this Helper," the Lord Jesus Christ, "who will, in the long run, be satisfied with nothing less than absolute perfection, will also be delighted with the first feeble, stumbling effort you make tomorrow to do the simplest duty. As a great Christian writer (George McDonald) pointed out, every father is pleased at the baby' s first attempt to walk [though] no father would be satisfied with anything less than a firm, manly walk in a grown-up son. In the same way, he said, 'God is easy to please, but hard to satisfy.' "[6] The process may take time. But the determination to follow the Master, the commitment to submit to him, the desire to partake of his goodness and grace—these things may begin in an instant, suddenly, as our hearts cry out for that life which is in Christ. Discipleship begins with a decision.

NOTES

1. Joseph Smith, *Lectures on Faith* (Salt Lake City: Deseret Book Co., 1985), 6:7.

2. John F. MacArthur, Jr., *The Gospel According to Jesus* (Grand Rapids, Mich.: Zondervan, 1988), p. 184.

3. MacArthur, *Gospel According to Jesus,* p. 182.

4. In Conference Report, Oct. 1974, p. 44.

5. George Albert Smith, *Sharing the Gospel with Others,* comp. Preston Nibley (Salt Lake City: Deseret Book Co., 1948), pp. 42–43.

6. *Mere Christianity* (New York: Macmillan, 1952), p. 172.

Chapter 3

TAKE UPON YOU
THE NAME OF CHRIST

There is a name which is above every other name. It is a name by which all things were created, by which the heavens and the earth exist and continue. It is the only name under heaven by which salvation comes, by which men and women are justified of sin, sanctified from sin, and redeemed to eternal glory. It is the blessed name of Jesus. It is the name disciples take, the name by which they are known.

When Adam and Eve were cast from the Garden of Eden, they called upon God by prayer, even though they had become subject to spiritual death. They received a commandment to offer sacrifice of the firstlings of their flocks. "And Adam was obedient unto the commandments of the Lord. And after many days an angel of the Lord appeared unto Adam, saying: Why dost thou offer sacrifices unto the Lord? And Adam said unto him: I know not, save the Lord commanded me. And then the angel spake, saying: This thing is a similitude of the sacrifice of the Only Begotten of the Father, which is full of grace and truth." And then the angel sounded the clarion call, the commandment of commandments: "Wherefore, thou shalt *do all that thou doest in the name of the Son,* and thou shalt repent and call upon God in the name of the Son forevermore" (Moses 5:4–8; emphasis added). "All that thou doest."

All. The follower of the risen Lord is called upon to grapple with and comply with this divine directive: "all that thou doest." Disciples who are in the line of their duty are to gauge their

13

speech, their feelings, their attitudes, their behavior—all that they do—by this glorious standard. In short, as the agents of Jesus Christ, disciples are to seek with all their heart to represent their exalted Principal with dignity and propriety.

We take the name of Christ through being born again. "Being born again," said Joseph Smith, "comes by the Spirit of God through ordinances."[1] By exercising faith in Jesus Christ, repenting of sins, being baptized by water, and then living worthy of the companionship and sanctifying influence of the Holy Ghost, we are born again. We die as pertaining to the old ways of sin and come to live again, as new creatures, in regard to the things of righteousness. Those who experience this new birth enter into a new family relationship. They become the sons and daughters of Jesus Christ; Christ becomes the father of salvation, the source and substance of their new life. By the power of the Holy Ghost they begin to see things from Christ's point of view, to feel things as he does, to do as he does, even to receive his image in their countenances (Alma 5:14). And they take his name, the name of Christ. By it they are called and known. They become Christians in the truest sense.

Being born again and thereby taking the name of Christ are not just nice things to do. They are absolutely necessary. They are essential to true discipleship. Having returned from the agonies and sufferings of an abbreviated hell, Alma testified: "I have repented of my sins, and have been redeemed of the Lord; behold I am born of the Spirit. And the Lord said unto me: Marvel not that all mankind, yea, men and women, all nations, kindreds, tongues and people, must be born again; yea, born of God, changed from their carnal and fallen state, to a state of righteousness, being redeemed of God, becoming his sons and daughters; and thus they become new creatures; and unless they do this, they can in no wise inherit the kingdom of God" (Mosiah 27:24–26; compare Moses 6:58–60). Those who remain in the world of sin, who wander in the broad paths and refuse to come unto Christ—these are they who are lost and alone, familyless, nameless. They are spiritual orphans. Alma thus taught the

14

people of Zarahemla that "the good shepherd doth call you; yea, and in his own name he doth call you, which is the name of Christ; and if ye will not hearken unto the voice of the good shepherd, to the name by which ye are called, behold, ye are not the sheep of the good shepherd. And now if ye are not the sheep of the good shepherd, of what fold are ye? Behold, I say unto you, that the devil is your shepherd, and ye are of his fold" (Alma 5:38–39). The Lord explained in our day: "Behold, Jesus Christ is the name which is given of the Father, and there is none other name given whereby man can be saved; wherefore, all men must take upon them the name which is given of the Father, for in that name shall they be called at the last day; wherefore, if they know not the name by which they are called, they cannot have place in the kingdom of my Father" (D&C 18:23–25).

True disciples do not travel along the path to eternal life very long before they sense the significance and seriousness of speaking and acting in the name of Christ. To take his name — in prayers, in blessings, and even in sermons — is to act by a divine investiture of authority, to do or say what our blessed Lord would do and say under the same circumstances. Thus it is that to use his name frivolously or lightly, to do something in the name of Jesus Christ that is unbecoming or inappropriate, is to take his name in vain and to come under divine censure. "Behold," the Savior declared in a modern revelation, "I am Alpha and Omega, even Jesus Christ. Wherefore, let all men beware how they take my name in their lips — for behold, verily I say, that *many there be who are under this condemnation, who use the name of the Lord, and use it in vain, having not authority*" (D&C 63:60–62; emphasis added).

In the ultimate sense, we take the name of Deity now on a conditional basis, in preparation for a great day when the name of God — placed upon our foreheads symbolically — will be granted permanently. Thus Elder Dallin H. Oaks explained: "It is significant that when we partake of the sacrament we do not witness that we take upon us the name of Jesus Christ. We witness that we are willing to do so. (See D&C 20:77.) The fact that we only witness to our willingness suggests that something else must happen before we actually take that sacred name upon us in the most important sense." Further, "in this sense, our witness relates to some future event or status whose attainment is not self-assumed, but depends on the authority or initiative of the Savior himself."[2]

That future event is surely the time when the Lord seals his disciples to eternal life, when he grants unto them the blessings of exaltation, "which glory shall be a fulness and a continuation of the seeds forever and ever" (D&C 132:19). That future status is godhood. In that day "the Lamb shall stand upon Mount Zion, and with him a hundred and forty-four thousand, having his Father's name written on their foreheads" (D&C 133:18; Rev. 14:1). That group of one-hundred forty-four thousand high priests (see D&C 77:11), but representative of all who so attain, have the sacred name—meaning the title, the power, the glory, and the status—sealed upon them forevermore. These are they who are Gods, even the sons of God (D&C 76:58).

Disciples of Christ reverence and adore their Master. They know that there is power in the name, a name which represents the honor and glory of the Lord God Omnipotent. To follow Christ is to be true and faithful to the gospel covenant, to honor the sacred name under which we serve. It is to be a Christian.

<hr>

NOTES

1. *Teachings of the Prophet Joseph Smith,* sel. Joseph Fielding Smith (Salt Lake City: Deseret Book Co., 1976), p. 162.
2. In Conference Report, Apr. 1985, pp. 102, 105.

Chapter 4

TAKE MY YOKE UPON YOU

To come unto Christ is to come out of the world. It is to leave behind the world we once knew. Broad roads lead to Babylon. We arrive in Zion, the place of the pure in heart, only by navigating a strait and narrow path. The gospel invitation is not only an entreaty to let the Savior come into our lives but an appeal and a command to repent and follow the only perfect Being to walk the earth. Though the Savior came to earth on a search and rescue mission, he came to save us from, not in, our sins (Alma 11:37; Hel. 5:10).

"Come unto me," the Lord pleaded, "all ye that labour and are heavy laden, and I will give you rest. Take my yoke upon you, and learn of me; for I am meek and lowly in heart: and ye shall find rest unto your souls. For my yoke is easy, and my burden is light" (Matt. 11:28–30). A thoughtful New Testament scholar has written: "Jesus' hearers understood that the yoke was a symbol of submission. In the land of Israel yokes were made of wood, carefully fashioned by the carpenter's hand to fit the neck of the animal that was to wear it. Undoubtedly Jesus had made many yokes as a boy in Joseph's carpenter shop in Nazareth. This was a perfect illustration for salvation. The yoke worn by the animal to pull a load was used by the master to direct the animal.

"The yoke also signified discipleship. When our Lord added the phrase 'and learn from me,' the imagery would have been familiar to Jewish listeners. In ancient writings, a pupil who

17

submitted himself to a teacher was said to take the teacher's yoke."[1]

The Lord's yoke, his strengthening tie and lifeline to us, is customized—suited perfectly and precisely to those who in sincerity seek to follow him. Discipleship is personal, not competitive. Rather, he who knows the hearts and minds of men and women chooses the challenges and orchestrates the opportunities that will result in optimal learning and maximal development. To be yoked to Jesus is to be open to his tutorials, attentive to his lessons, intent finally on gaining "the mind of Christ" (1 Cor. 2:16).

There is no weight in life greater than the burden of sin. The Master beckons to us to unburden ourselves of the taints of a telestial world and adorn ourselves with the robes of righteousness. He invites us to shed the superficial, discard the ephemeral and the transient, and eschew the cheap and the gaudy. In addition, he pleads with his disciples to rise above the childish mentality that motivates people to do good for the sake of appearance or to seek salvation by their own unaided effort.

No doubt some of the greatest burdens we bear come from well-intended but misguided attempts to browbeat ourselves into righteousness. Some waste away their lives in anxiety and exhaustion, trying desperately to do it all themselves. In the meridian of time, Jesus offered hope and rest to the Jews, who were met on all sides by the taxing and ubiquitous requirements of the Law of Moses (see Acts 15:10); to these he promised alleviation of their guilt and liberation of their souls. In our day the Lord offers hope and rest to those who have tried every way but the right way to be good; to these he promises relief and comfort in return for their trust and reliance and continued faithfulness. His rest is the quiet assurance of divine approbation, that peace that comes from having been cleansed and filled.

The irony of our Lord's invitation lies in his statement that his yoke is easy and his burden light. The most onerous burden ever borne in eternity was borne by Christ. A universal fall necessitated a universal and infinite atonement, and Christ's

18

sufferings in Gethsemane and on Golgotha are beyond mortal comprehension. Truly, he descended below all things so that he (and those whom he would lift) might ascend above all things (see D&C 88:6; Eph. 4:8–10). The awful atonement thereby opened the way for us to rest; our burdens—borne by him—become light.

Some years ago Elder Boyd K. Packer spoke of visiting a county fair in New England. "The center of attraction was the oxen pulling contest. Several teams of oxen with heavy wooden yokes were lined up to compete. A wooden sledge was weighted with cement blocks: ten thousand pounds—five tons—to begin with. The object was for the oxen to move the sledge three feet.

"I noticed a well-matched pair of very large, brindled, blue-gray animals. They were the big-boned, Holstein, Durham-cross, familiar big blue oxen of seasons past. Because of their size, of course they were the favorites.

"Each team was given three attempts to move the sledge. If they were able to do so easily, more weight was added until the teams were eliminated one by one. In turn, each team was hitched to the sledge. The teamster would position his animals carefully, pat them, chortle to them, whisper to them, and then at a goad and a loud command they would slam forward against the yoke. Either the weight would move or the oxen were jerked to a halt.

"The big blue oxen didn't even place! A small, nondescript pair of animals, not very well matched for size, moved the sledge all three times.

"I was amazed and fascinated and turned to an old New Englander in the crowd and asked if he could explain how that could happen. . . . And then he explained. The big blues were larger and stronger and better matched for size than the other team. But the little oxen had better teamwork and coordination. They hit the yoke together. Both animals jerked forward at exactly the same time and the force moved the load.

"One of the big blue oxen had lagged a second or pushed a second too soon—something like a football player being off side—and the force was spent in a glancing blow. The yoke then

19

was twisted and the team jerked to one side and the sledge hardly moved.

"If I were to moralize, I would begin in typical Book of Mormon language, 'And thus we see' that size and strength are not enough. It takes teamwork as well."[2]

Success and happiness in this life will derive largely from our attitude toward the yoke of Christ. If we insist that we have a better idea, if we contend that we can handle all situations ourselves, if we choose alternate paths and convenient detours, then the yoke of Christ will become a coarse collar, a confining chain. If, however, we submit to Christ, offer our whole souls as an offering unto him (Omni 1:26), and yield to the enticings and promptings of his Holy Spirit, then we shall come to glory in the freedom — rejoice in the liberty — that comes in and through his love and mercies and condescensions. "The yoke of the law," one commentator has explained, "the yoke of human effort, the yoke of works, and the yoke of sin are all heavy, chafing, galling yokes. They represent large, unbearable burdens carried in the flesh. They lead to despair, frustration, and anxiety. Jesus offers a yoke we can carry, and He also gives the strength to carry it.

"The yoke He offers is easy, and the burden He carries is light, because He is meek and lowly. Unlike the Pharisees and scribes, He does not desire to oppress us. He does not want to pile burdens on us we cannot bear, nor is he trying to show how hard righteousness can be. He is gentle. He is tender. And He gives a light burden to carry. Obedience under His yoke is a joy. It is when we disobey that the yoke chafes our neck."[3]

"Peace I leave with you," said the Prince of Peace, "my peace I give unto you: not as the world giveth, give I unto you. Let not your heart be troubled, neither let it be afraid" (John 14:27). Indeed, compliance with his terms, his conditions, and the requirements of his gospel covenant — all of which are given to strengthen and sanctify us — leads to freedom. "If ye continue in my word," the Redeemer counseled, "then are ye my disciples indeed; and ye shall know the truth, and the truth shall make you free" (John 8:31–32). Thus abiding in the liberty whereby we are made free (D&C 88:86), "the peace of God, which passeth all understanding, shall keep [our] hearts and minds through Christ Jesus" (Phil. 4:7). Our souls are at rest.

NOTES

1. John F. MacArthur, Jr., *The Gospel According to Jesus* (Grand Rapids, Mich.: Zondervan, 1988), p. 112.

2. "Equally Yoked Together," in *Charge to Religious Educators*, 2d ed. (Salt Lake City: The Church of Jesus Christ of Latter-day Saints, 1982), p. 27.

3. MacArthur, *Gospel According to Jesus*, p. 113.

THE COST OF DISCIPLESHIP

Chapter 5

HE THAT LOSETH HIS LIFE

Following Christ entails looking to him. It means seeing to the welfare of others in his name. In the process—and the joy of discipleship is as much in the process, the journey, as it is in the destination—Christians discover and find themselves. In that regard the Master uttered one of the most profound ironies of the ages when he taught: "He who seeketh to save his life shall lose it; and he who loseth his life for my sake shall find it" (JST, Matt. 10:34).

It is the natural man that seeks acclaim, that requires attention, that elicits compliments, that feasts upon praise. It is the man or woman who is "without God in the world," who is "in a state of nature," who has "gone contrary to the nature of God" and thus the nature of happiness—it is this person who is so busy taking the emotional temperature, so anxious to be fulfilled. "The natural life in each of us," C. S. Lewis wrote, "is something self-centered, something that wants to be petted and admired. . . .

"And especially it wants to be left to itself: to keep well away from anything better or stronger or higher than it, anything that might make it feel small. It is afraid of the light and air of the spiritual world, just as people who have been brought up to be dirty are afraid of a bath. And in a sense it is quite right. It knows that if the spiritual life gets hold of it, all its self-centeredness and self-will are going to be killed and it is ready to fight tooth and nail to avoid that."[1]

To be sure, the natural man need not be degenerate, a vicious personality, a lewd fellow of the baser sort, a criminal. In a real sense, however, all of us are natural men until we accept the revealed witness of the truth and are cleansed from our fallen condition through the atoning blood of Christ, by the power of the Holy Ghost. In that condition, desiring to please the Master and to do his will, disciples of Christ begin to forsake their own agenda and to learn and abide by the will of their Principal. Putting off the natural man (Mosiah 3:19) thus entails, among other things, the gradual acquisition of a pure heart. One with a pure heart is unconcerned about power or fame or notoriety; he finds pleasure in simple things, joy in the ordinary. Again from C. S. Lewis: "The more you obey your conscience, the more your conscience will demand of you. And your natural self, which is thus being starved and hampered and worried at every turn, will get angrier and angrier. It is as though Jesus were saying to each of us: 'Give me All. I don't want so much of your time and so much of your money and so much of your work: I want You. I have not come to torment your natural self, but to kill it. . . . Hand over the whole natural self. . . . I will give you a new self instead. In fact, I will give you Myself: my own will shall become yours.' "[2]

In one sense, then, a person loses himself when he finds Christ, the Captain of his soul. He loses himself when he becomes less obsessed with personal whims, more directed toward divine design. She loses herself when she is willing, without let or hindrance, to dedicate herself to the Church of Jesus Christ and to labor with fidelity to assist in the establishment of the kingdom of God on earth. Luke recorded the Savior's words as follows: "For whosoever will save his life, must be willing to lose it for my sake; and whosoever will be willing to lose his life for my sake the same shall save it. For *what doth it profit a man if he gain the whole world, and yet he receive him not whom God hath ordained*, and he lose his own soul, and he himself be a castaway?" (JST, Luke 9:24–25; emphasis added).

The disciple loses his life when he serves his fellowman,

when he places others' comfort and convenience before his own. Our Exemplar said: "I am among you as he that serveth" (Luke 22:27). King Benjamin thus instructed his people that "when ye are in the service of your fellow beings ye are only in the service of your God" (Mosiah 2:17). President Harold B. Lee shared with the Church an experience that illustrates that vital principle: "It was just before the dedication of the Los Angeles Temple. We were all preparing for that great occasion. It was something new in my life, when along about three or four o'clock in the morning, I enjoyed an experience that I think was not a dream, but it must have been a vision. It seemed that I was witnessing a great spiritual gathering, where men and women were standing up, two or three at a time, and speaking in tongues. The Spirit was so unusual. I seemed to have heard the voice of President David O. McKay say, *"If you want to love God, you have to learn to love and serve the people. That is the way you show your love for God."*[3]

Service sanctifies both giver and receiver. Those who involve themselves in the work of the Master receive the approbation of the Master. Peter taught that charity prevents a multitude of sins (JST, 1 Pet. 4:8). James likewise wrote that "he which converteth the sinner from the error of his way shall save a soul from death, and shall hide a multitude of [his own] sins" (James 5:20; compare D&C 84:61). Indeed, it is through searching out (being sensitive to) and seeing to the needs of the poor—both temporally and spiritually—that disciples of Christ are able to maintain their spiritual standing before their Maker, to retain a remission of sins from day to day (Mosiah 4:11–12, 26).

In the ultimate sense, disciples are willing to give their own life—to face death—in the cause of truth if such is required. Here pretense and appearance fade away rapidly; no person in his right mind would offer to suffer death for a cause to which he or she was not absolutely committed. As Joseph Smith taught: "For a man to lay down his all, his character and reputation, his honor, and applause, his good name among men, his houses, his lands, his brothers and sisters, his wife and children, and even his own life also—counting all things but filth and dross for the excellency of the knowledge of Jesus Christ—requires more than mere belief or supposition that he is doing the will of God."[4]

It is not easy to die, even to die in the faith. No one wants to die, even to die the death of a martyr. And yet how else could the Lord obtain that unconditional dedication from his people so necessary to the perpetuation of a system of salvation that spans the veil? Certainly the scriptures do not "teach salvation by martyrdom. The Lord was not advising the disciples to try to get themselves killed for Him. . . . He simply says that genuine Christians do not shrink back, even in the face of death. To express it another way, the true disciple tends to follow the Lord, even at the expense of his own self."[5] But should such be necessary, the reward is at least as great as the cost: "Let no man be afraid to lay down his life for my sake; for whoso layeth down his life for my sake shall find it again" On the other hand, "whoso is not willing to lay down his life for my sake is not my disciple" (D&C 103:27–28). And what reward shall the follower of the Nazarene find? "Whoso layeth down his life in my cause, for my name's sake, shall find it again, even life eternal" (D&C 98:13; compare 101:15, 35).

One of the sad commentaries of this modern age is that so many have lost the way—the way to happiness, the way to genuine fulfillment, the way to peace. It just may be that those who work hardest at trying to find themselves—at least according to the world's standards and methods—will, unfortunately, continue to wander in the morass of existential anguish. For, in the words of the Prophet Joseph Smith, "If men do not comprehend the character of God, they do not comprehend themselves."[6] Those who turn to the Lord and enter into covenant with him find themselves and make their way along that strait and narrow path which leads to the abundant life. That life is worth whatever paltry price we have had to pay along the way, and in the end we shall see that there really was no sacrifice at all.

NOTES

1. *Mere Christianity* (New York: Macmillan, 1952), p. 154.

2. *Mere Christianity*, pp. 166–67.

3. In Conference Report, Apr. 1973, p. 180; emphasis added.

4. Joseph Smith, *Lectures on Faith* (Salt Lake City: Deseret Book Co., 1985), 6:5.

5. John F. MacArthur, Jr., *The Gospel According to Jesus* (Grand Rapids, Mich.: Zondervan, 1988), p. 202.

6. *Teachings of the Prophet Joseph Smith*, sel. Joseph Fielding Smith (Salt Lake City: Deseret Book Co., 1976), p. 343.

Chapter 6

WHAT WILL A MAN GIVE IN EXCHANGE FOR HIS SOUL?

Is anything in this life worth my soul? Is there any reward, any honor, any mortal station that is so deserving of my attention and my affections that I would mortgage my eternal future for them? How much is a soul worth? Can it be purchased? Traded away? Is a modern mess of pottage so appealing as to cause me to forfeit my place at the banquet of the Bridegroom? Is the devil's first article of faithlessness—that anything in this world can be acquired with money—really true, as so many contend?

We need not kneel at the shrines of wooden or stone gods to be idolatrous. We need not offer sacrifice to a lifeless deity to have forsaken the faith of our fathers. Rather, we need only devote the bulk of our time, talents, and means to the establishment or proliferation of a cause other than the gospel cause. False objects of adoration and worship may in our day take the form of real estate or portfolios or chrome or furniture or leisure, none of which is innately evil but which as ends in themselves— rather than means—consume and corrupt. Any time *things* take precedence over persons, particularly the Person of Christ, we are on a downward spiral of personal apostasy. We have wandered off the path of the disciple.

The Book of Mormon is a powerful witness that "wealth is a jealous master who will not be served half-heartedly and will suffer no rival—not even God." Tragically, "the more important wealth is, the less important it is how one gets it."[1] Mammon, or money, is indeed a tyrannical master. It demands center stage;

30

it beckons to be afforded prominence as an all-consuming passion. The craving for it is insatiable. Wants are gradually transformed into needs. Values are gradually diluted and then dissolved.

The scriptures record that there came to Jesus on one occasion a young man who sought the blessings of eternal life. He inquired of the Savior what was expected of him to achieve that end. The Lord detailed a number of the commandments, which he himself had delivered to Moses on Sinai. The response from the young man was, "All these things have I observed from my youth." Mark adds tenderly: "Then Jesus beholding him loved him" — for the fellow was a good man, a faithful man — "and said unto him, One thing thou lackest: go thy way, sell whatsoever thou hast, and give to the poor, and thou shalt have treasure in heaven: and come, take up the cross, and follow me." And then comes the poignant moment of truth: "And he [the young man] was sad at that saying, and went away grieved: for he had great possessions" (Mark 10:17–22).

A Protestant commentator, John MacArthur, offered the following insight into this sad scenario: Jesus "challenged his claim to having kept the law. In effect, Christ told the young man, 'You say you love your neighbor as yourself. OK, give him everything you've got. If you really love him as much as you love yourself, that should be no problem.'

"Here is the ultimate test: will this man obey the Lord? Jesus is not teaching salvation by philanthropy. He is not saying it is possible to buy eternal life with charity. But He is saying, 'Are you going to do what I want you to do? Who will run your life, you or I?' The Lord put his finger on the very nerve of this man's existence. Knowing where his heart was, He said, 'Unless I can be the highest authority in your life, there's no salvation for you.' By placing Himself alongside the man's wealth and demanding he make the choice, our Lord revealed the true state of the young man's heart.

"Do we literally have to give away everything we own to become Christians? No, but we do have to be willing to forsake

31

all (Luke 14:33), meaning we cling to nothing that takes precedence over Christ. We must be eager to do whatever he asks. . . . The Lord made a frontal attack on the man's weakness—the sin of covetousness, indulgence, and materialism."[2]

"We might well ask," Elder Bruce R. McConkie observed, " 'Isn't it enough to keep the commandments? What more is expected of us than to be true and faithful to every trust? Is there more than the law of obedience?'

"In the case of our rich young friend there was more. He was expected to live the law of consecration. . . . We are left to wonder what intimacies he might have shared with the Son of God, what fellowship he might have enjoyed with the apostles, what revelations and visions he might have received, if he had been able to live the law of a celestial kingdom. As it is he remains nameless; as it might have been, his name could have been had in honorable remembrance among the saints forever."[3]

The pitiable plight of those who trust in their riches is a type of moral myopia, a growing and blatant insensitivity to those who have less than they. In short, we can hardly notice the needy about us when our eye is single to ourselves—when we are possessed of a type of arrogant aggrandizement—and when our thoughts and feelings are preoccupied with getting more of what we already have. Surely there are few more serious setbacks to our discipleship than coveting our own property (see D&C 19:26). Didn't someone warn us once:

"Take heed, and beware of covetousness: for a man's life consisteth not in the abundance of the things which he possesseth"? He then uttered a hard saying in the form of a parable:

"And he spake a parable unto them, saying, The ground of a certain rich man brought forth plentifully: and he thought within himself, saying, What shall I do, because I have no room where to bestow my fruits? And he said, This will I do: I will pull down my barns, and build greater; and there will I bestow all my fruits and my goods. And I will say to my soul, Soul, thou hast much goods laid up for many years; take thine ease, eat, drink, and be merry. But God said unto him, Thou fool, this night thy soul shall be required of thee: then whose shall those things be, which thou hast provided?"

And then the precept to be pondered: "So is he that layeth up treasure for himself, and is not rich toward God" (Luke 12:15–21). Some things simply will not be permitted through celestial customs.

Ananias and Sapphira — and the Saints of their day — learned a lesson long to be remembered. Having voluntarily entered into covenant to consecrate all they had to the Lord through the legal administrators, they secretly determined upon a plan to assure a style of living to which they had become accustomed: they "kept back" a portion of their property. But Simon Peter, moved upon by that Spirit which searcheth the hearts and thus knoweth all things (Rom. 8:27; D&C 42:17), confronted the deceptive duo with the penetrating words: "Why hath Satan filled thine heart to lie to the Holy Ghost. . . . ? Why hast thou conceived this thing in thine heart? Thou hast not lied unto men, but unto God." Both Ananias and Sapphira, exposed in their hypocrisy, fell dead at the feet of the apostles. "And great fear came upon all the church, and upon as many as heard these things" (Acts 5:1–11).

This story is harsh and dramatic. Its lesson is frightening. And it is unusual, for seldom does God strike one dead for hypocrisy. It is, however, accurate and descriptive, symbolic, if you will, of the spiritual death and alienation from things of righteousness that surely shall be for all who follow such a course.

Jesus said what he meant and meant what he said when he taught that it is easier for a camel to go through the eye of a needle than for a rich man to enter into the kingdom of heaven. There is no metaphor intended. No softening of this hard saying by linguistic or cultural traditions is justifiable. The Savior said what he said. "Who then can be saved?" the apostles asked. "With men that trust in riches, it is impossible; but not impossible with men who trust in God and leave all for my sake, for with such all things are possible" (JST, Mark 10:22–26; compare JST,

Matt. 19:26; JST, Luke 18:27). The issue, then, is one of trust. Reliance. Dependence. The Almighty, who promises us all that he has, asks simply that we be willing to give him all. Nothing else will do.

It is not that the Lord does not want his people to prosper. In fact, "It is not important that I should have no possessions, but if I do I must keep them as though I had them not, in other words I must cultivate a spirit of inward detachment, so that my heart is not in my possessions."[4] The anxiety against which the Savior warns his disciples (Matt. 6:25) is concerned with future times, with my goods, with my holdings, with my ability to provide adequately. Truly "the way to misuse our possessions is to use them as an insurance against the morrow. Anxiety is always directed to the morrow, whereas goods are in the strictest sense meant to be used only for today. By trying to ensure for the next day we are only creating uncertainty today. . . . The only way to win assurance is by leaving tomorrow entirely in the hands of God and by receiving from him all we need for today."[5]

As the disciple grows in discernment and in spiritual sensitivity, he or she comes to cherish those things that matter most and to ignore or eschew those that appeal to the senses but do little to settle and soothe the soul. The disciple begins to appreciate the counsel of a modern seer: "You need not be either rich or hold high position to be completely successful and truly happy," said Elder Boyd K. Packer. "In fact, if these things come to you, and they may, true success must be achieved in spite of them, not because of them." He continued: "The choice of life is not between fame and obscurity, nor is the choice between wealth and poverty. The choice is between good and evil, and that is a very different matter indeed."[6]

In a modern revelation the Lord explained that "the worth of souls is great in the sight of God" (D&C 18:10). Latter-day Saints are fond of quoting this verse and then skipping down the scriptural page to those verses that speak further of the joy that comes from bringing the blessings of the gospel into the lives of many. The question might be asked: *Why* is the worth of souls great? In the context of what we have been discussing, why is a soul so precious? Why is it so tragic to sell one's soul and in Faustian fashion trade away the unspeakable hereafter for the unthinkable here and now? We might respond that as children of the Man of Holiness we have marvelous possibilities. As sons and daughters of God, we are possessed (although now in rudimentary form) of the attributes of godliness. The Lord provides an additional answer from scripture: "For, behold, the Lord your Redeemer suffered death in the flesh; wherefore he suffered the pain of all men, that all men might repent and come unto him. And he hath risen again from the dead, that he might bring all men unto him, on conditions of repentance. And how great is his joy in the soul that repenteth! Wherefore, you are called to cry repentance unto this people" (D&C 18:11–14). Simply stated, the soul is of infinite worth. We are not our own. We have been bought with an infinite price (1 Cor. 6:19–20), even with "the precious blood of Christ, as of a lamb without blemish and without spot" (1 Pet. 1:19).

Through our Redeemer and Benefactor we may become "a chosen generation, a royal priesthood, an holy nation, a peculiar [purchased] people; that [we] should shew forth the praises of him who hath called [us] out of darkness into his marvelous light" (1 Pet. 2:9). From this perspective, then, our absolute commitment to the Lord is a fundamental expression of gratitude to Jesus Christ, who has ransomed us. It is a statement of appreciation. But our pure love for him also places us on a path, the path of the true disciple, which leads to limitless eternal privileges in the realms ahead. "Eye hath not seen, nor ear heard, neither have entered into the heart of man, the things which God hath prepared for them that love him" (1 Cor. 2:9).

NOTES

1. Hugh Nibley, *Since Cumorah* (Salt Lake City: Deseret Book Co., 1976), pp. 393–94.

2. John F. MacArthur, Jr., *The Gospel According to Jesus* (Grand Rapids, Mich.: Zondervan, 1988), pp. 86–87.

3. In Conference Report, Apr. 1975, pp. 75–76.

4. Dietrich Bonhoeffer, *The Cost of Discipleship*, rev. ed. (New York: Macmillan, 1963), p. 88.

5. Bonhoeffer, *Cost of Discipleship*, pp. 197–98.

6. In Conference Report, Oct. 1980, pp. 28–29.

Chapter 7

TAKE UP YOUR CROSS

Jesus is our pattern, our example. He bids us to follow him, to walk where he has trod. To enjoy fellowship with him and his Spirit, we must be prepared to face the alienation and loneliness of well doing; submit to the tauntings and abuse of a world that grossly misunderstands our intentions; and, if called upon so to do, walk through the valley of the shadow of death without fear or hesitation. Jesus—the great Jehovah, the God of Abraham, Isaac, and Jacob—"humbled himself, and became obedient unto death, even the death of the cross" (Phil. 2:8). He who did all things well, who gained the mastery over life and death, even he bids us to traverse a similar path. He calls us to take up our own crosses and follow where he has led. Our Lord points out that "whosoever doth not bear his cross, and come after me, cannot be my disciple" (Luke 14:27; compare Matt. 10:38; Mark 8:34).

Though the atonement of Jesus Christ was accomplished both in the Garden of Gethsemane and on the hill of Calvary, Christians around the world frequently speak of that central act of reconciliation as "the cross of Christ." Even the Savior himself so speaks. While among his American Hebrews, Jesus explained: "Behold I have given unto you my gospel, and this is the gospel which I have given unto you—that I came into the world to do the will of my Father, because my Father sent me. And *my Father sent me that I might be lifted up upon the cross*; and after that I had been lifted up upon the cross, that I might draw all men unto me, that as I have been lifted up by men even so should men be lifted up by the Father, to stand before me, to be judged of their works, whether they be good or whether they be evil" (3 Ne. 27:13–14; emphasis added). It might also be appropriate to refer to the Lord's condescension — his temptations and pain and sufferings — throughout his mortal life as his cross. In this sense our Master carried his cross before and after Gethsemane.

There is a sense in which we as disciples take up our cross by applying the atoning blood of Christ, by repenting and coming unto him. Thus the death of the natural man is followed by the birth of the spiritual man and the rise to a newness of life. "Our old man is crucified with him," Paul said, "that the body of sin might be destroyed, that henceforth we should not serve sin" (Rom. 6:6). To the Galatians Paul likewise taught: "I am crucified with Christ: nevertheless, I live; yet not I, but Christ liveth in me" (Gal. 2:20). From the Christian perspective, then, our earthly stains were affixed (with our Savior) to Golgotha's cross (see Col. 2:14). President Joseph F. Smith thus reminded us that "having been born anew, which is the putting away of the old man sin, and putting on of the man Christ Jesus, we have become soldiers of the Cross, having enlisted under the banner of Jehovah for time and for eternity"[1]

We take up our cross as we seek to put down our sins and thereby enter the realm of divine experience. Thus Jesus instructed those who desired discipleship: "If any man will come after me, let him deny himself, and take up his cross and follow me. And now *for a man to take up his cross, is to deny himself all ungodliness, and every worldly lust, and keep my commandments*" (JST, Matt. 16:25–26; emphasis added). Having called the Nephites to a higher righteousness than that put forward in the Law, having cautioned them specifically against immorality, Jesus said: "Behold, I give unto you a commandment, that ye suffer none of these things to enter into your heart; for it is better that ye should deny yourselves of these things, wherein ye will take up your cross, than that ye should be cast into hell" (3 Ne. 12:29–30). It is presumably in this sense that Alma counseled his

38

errant son Corianton: "Now my son, I would that ye should repent and forsake your sins, and go no more after the lusts of your eyes, but *cross yourself* in all these things; for except ye do this ye can in nowise inherit the kingdom of God. Oh, remember, and take it upon you, and *cross yourself* in these things" (Alma 39:9; emphasis added).

There is another way in which disciples are expected to take up their cross. It may well be one of the most difficult labors of the Christian, but our involvement in this work makes us more like the Merciful One than anything else we might do. The German theologian Dietrich Bonhoeffer observed:

"While it is true that only the sufferings of Christ are a means of atonement, yet since he has suffered for and borne the sins of the whole world and shares with his disciples the fruits of his passion [sufferings], the Christian also has to undergo temptation, he too has to bear the sins of others; he too must bear their shame and be driven like a scapegoat from the gate of the city. But he would certainly break down under this burden, but for the support of him who bore the sins of all. The passion of Christ strengthens him to overcome the sins of others by forgiving them. He becomes the bearer of other men's burdens. . . . *My brother's burden which I must bear is not only his outward lot, his natural characteristics and gifts, but quite literally his sin. And the only way to bear that sin is by forgiving it in the power of the cross of Christ in which I now share.*"

Summing up, "The call to follow Christ always means a call to share the work of forgiving men their sins. Forgiveness is the Christlike suffering which it is the Christian's duty to bear."[2] To modern disciples in his restored Church the Lord thus instructed: "I, the Lord will forgive whom I will forgive, but of you it is required to forgive all men" (D&C 64:10).

In some ways, the call to discipleship is also a call to suffer. It is a call to bear with the trials of this life and particularly the indifference or rejection of those who despise the way of holiness. To go where Christ has gone we must be willing—at least in part—to bear what he has borne. To inherit celestial glory we must be willing to face the refining fires of suffering. The Apostle Peter encouraged the Saints of his day: "Beloved, think it not strange concerning the fiery trial which is to try you, as though some strange thing happened unto you: but rejoice, inasmuch as ye are partakers of Christ's sufferings; that, when his glory shall be revealed, ye may be glad also with exceeding joy" (1 Pet. 4:12–13). Paul counseled the Roman Saints in the same vein. "The Spirit itself beareth witness with our spirit," he said, "that we are the children of God: and if children, then heirs; heirs of God, and *joint-heirs with Jesus Christ; if so be that we suffer with him, that we may be also glorified together*" (Rom. 8:16–17; emphasis added). Indeed, to some degree we gain fellowship with Him only through participating in what Paul called "the fellowship of his suffering." In his epistle to the Philippians, he stated: "I count all things but loss for the excellency of the knowledge of Christ Jesus my Lord: for whom I have suffered the loss of all things, and do count them but dung, that I may win Christ, . . . that I may know him, and the power of his resurrection, and the fellowship of his sufferings, being made conformable unto his death" (Philip. 3:8, 10).

The ungodly, and in some cases even the spiritually inexperienced, regard the path of discipleship as foolishness. Because they do not know, they assume that no one does. Because they do not feel, they generalize from their own spiritual void to their fellows. And, typically, what people are not up on, they tend to be down on. Righteousness and certitude are anathema to the agnostic, and thus true believers are scoffed or scorned for their testimonies. The disciple must be prepared to withstand the taunts of the ignorant, as well as the attacks of the perverse. Paul encouraged the Saints to "run with patience the race that is set before us, looking unto Jesus the author and finisher of our faith; who for the joy that was set before him endured the cross, *despising the shame*, and is set down at the right hand of the throne of God" (Heb. 12:1–2; emphasis added). That is to say, Jesus paid little attention to those who sought to shame him, who sought to embarrass or ridicule him for his teachings and way of life. Nephi observed that in his father's dream-vision of the tree of life, the people in the great and spacious building "did point the finger of scorn at me and those that were partaking of the fruit also; but *we heeded them not*" (1 Ne. 8:33; emphasis added). Jacob issued a marvelous challenge in what is certainly an experiential verse: "Wherefore, we would to God that we could persuade all men not to rebel against God, to provoke him to anger, but that all men would believe in Christ, and view his death, and suffer his cross and bear the shame of the world" (Jacob 1:8).

Taking up our cross is thus not something which takes place in a single instance, nor is it necessarily one great and final test of our discipleship. We do not work out our salvation in a day or an instant, and we generally do not pass the tests of mortality through one episode of courage or one occasion of exceptional bravery. Salvation is a process. Discipleship is a process. And taking up our cross is something we do regularly and consistently. Luke therefore records Jesus' words as follows: "If any man will come after me, let him deny himself, and *take up his cross daily*, and follow me" (Luke 9:23; emphasis added). And so it is that "a true believer is one who signs up for life."

"The bumper-sticker sentiment, 'Try Jesus,' is a mentality foreign to real discipleship—faith is not an experiment but a lifelong commitment. It means taking up the cross daily, giving all for Christ each day with no reservations, no uncertainty, no hesitation. It means nothing is knowingly held back, nothing purposely shielded from His lordship, nothing stubbornly kept from His control. It calls for a painful severing of the tie with the world, a sealing of the escape hatches, a ridding oneself of any kind of security to fall back on in case of failure. A genuine believer knows he is going ahead with Christ until death."[3]

And so the ever-present and persistent reminder regarding the cost of discipleship in every age and time is, "He that will not take up his cross and follow me, and keep my commandments, the same shall not be saved" (D&C 56:2). The followers of Christ walk in the steps of their Master. The road is long, and the climb is tiresome and hazardous. The compensation, however, that which awaits the faithful, is sublime. Jacob thus exulted that "the righteous, the saints of the Holy One of Israel, they who have believed in the Holy One of Israel, they who have endured the crosses of the world, and despised the shame of it, they shall inherit the kingdom of God, which was prepared for them from the foundation of the world, and their joy shall be full forever" (2 Ne. 9:18).

NOTES

1. *Gospel Doctrine* (Salt Lake City: Deseret Book Co., 1971), p. 91.

2. *The Cost of Discipleship*, rev. ed. (New York: Macmillan, 1963), p. 100; emphasis added.

3. John F. MacArthur, Jr., *The Gospel According to Jesus* (Grand Rapids, Mich.: Zondervan, 1988), p. 202.

Chapter 8

THE SALT OF THE EARTH

The Lord calls us to make a difference in the world. Things simply ought to be better because we are present. In reality, we can only make a difference if we are different. Not necessarily strange. Different. Indeed, disciples of Christ are to stand in stark contrast to those who conform, concede, and thereby compromise.

As a part of his Sermon on the Mount, Jesus taught: "Verily, verily, I say unto you, I give unto you to be the salt of the earth; but if the salt shall lose its savor, wherewith shall the earth be salted? the salt shall thenceforth be good for nothing, but to be cast out, and to be trodden under foot of men" (JST, Matt. 5:15). That the Lord had specific reference to his disciples—to baptized members of the Church who have received him and his gospel by covenant—is affirmed in a modern revelation. "When men are called into mine everlasting gospel," the Savior said in 1833, "and covenant with an everlasting covenant, they are accounted as the salt of the earth and the savor of men; they are called to be the savor of men" (D&C 101:39–40). One Bible commentator has observed: "Seasoning [in antiquity] was limited to salt, obtainable from the endless supplies in the salt hills near the Dead Sea. It was used to flavour and preserve food (Job 6:6). In New Testament times there was a thriving industry based at Magdala, where fish were salted and exported. Not until Greek and Roman times were other seasonings (spices) readily available, and this developed as trade grew."[1] The Saints are asked to stand as a spice, a seasoning, a flavor among the bland and often tasteless elements of the world. Because they are there, things are better; like salt, the people of the Lord are empowered to bring out the best in others.

Anciently salt was believed to have healing properties (see 2 Kgs. 2:19–22). In addition, it had an important place in sacrificial offerings (Lev. 2:13), which may have been related to the Old Testament custom of using salt in a meal in which participants celebrated the signing of an agreement (see Num. 18:19). Further, "meals were an important aspect of friendship. To eat a meal with someone was to be at peace with him (Gen. 26:28–30). Salt had a particular function as part of the meal. To 'eat salt' was to be at peace—perhaps because it healed wounds." Thus "when Jesus tells us to be 'salty,' he is therefore telling us to be at peace with others."[2] Those who have taken upon them the name of Christ—those who have received the Comforter by the laying on of hands—covenant to bear others' burdens, to mourn with those that mourn, and to comfort those who stand in need of comfort (see Mosiah 18:8–9). They have committed to be peace-makers, to be as oil on troubled waters, to serve as a soothing balm in the midst of calamity or controversy. They are as salt.

Salt is a preservative. It preserves food from corruption and keeps it wholesome and acceptable. The disciples are likewise called to be as preservatives on earth. They are called out of the world to stand as witnesses against creeping relativity and the dilution of time-honored values. They are summoned by the Savior to declare with love and boldness those principles of light and virtue, those absolute truths decreed by an all-wise God and his prophets. "Jesus calls [the disciples]," Bonhoeffer explained, "the salt of the earth—salt, the most indispensable necessity of life. The disciples, that is to say, are the highest good, the supreme value which the earth possesses, for without them it cannot live. . . . In casting out the disciples the earth is destroying its very life."[3] A modern revelation declared: "They [the Saints] were set to be a light unto the world, and to be the *saviors of men*; and inasmuch as they are not the saviors of men, they are as salt that has lost its savor" (D&C 103:9–10; emphasis added). We note with interest the number of times in scripture the Lord warns the wicked that inasmuch as they cast out the prophets and the righteous element from among them, they are ripe for destruction. To dispel the nucleus of faith is to sever the very lifeline which could pull them through the storms of life into a safe harbor (see Alma 10:22–23; Hel. 13:12).

And what of those who are called out of the world but differ but little from the world? What of those whose style of life, attitude, and manner of speaking is no different from the typical natural man? What of those who have lost their savor? Elder Carlos E. Asay explained that "salt will not lose its savor with age. Savor is lost *through mixture and contamination.* . . . Flavor and quality flee a man when he contaminates his mind with unclean thoughts, desecrates his mouth by speaking less than the truth, and misapplies his strength in performing evil acts."[4] Salt that does not flavor, heal, or preserve serves little useful function. It is no longer salt. It is fit only to be trodden underfoot. "When salt was collected from the Dead Sea area, some of it was good for salting and cooking, but other salt had lost its saltiness. This salt was not thrown away, however. It was stored in the Jerusalem Temple, and when the winter rains made the marble courtyards slippery, it was spread on them to reduce the slipperiness. Hence salt that has lost its saltiness is trodden under the foot of men."[5]

The way of the disciple is the way of holiness. It is a walk away from the ways of the world. It represents a genuine refinement of the soul, a cleansing of the inner self. Disciples who look ahead to that life which is in the Lord are far less prone to look back to the sinking standards of a sick society. Those who cherish virtue come to abhor vice. Those who are alive to the things of righteousness become dead to the ways of sin. And yet the Saints are invited to make their mark on society, to leaven the loaf. And so it is that only as they first come out of the world, come to Christ, be lifted and built up and fortified in him, may they then seek to lift and build up and fortify others against the

45

onslaught of avarice and the mountains of malevolence. Elder Asay counseled us regarding how to avoid mixture and contamination: "If it is not *clean*, do not think it; if it is not *true*, do not speak it; if it is not *good*, do not do it."[6]

The Savior's use of salt as a symbol of Christian discipleship is so very appropriate. What we are, deep down to the core, is so much more important than what we appear to be. Elder Bruce R. McConkie taught:

"In the final analysis, the gospel of God is written, not in the dead letters of scriptural records, but in the lives of the Saints. It is not written with pen and ink on paper of man's making, but with acts and deeds in the book of life of each believing and obedient person. It is engraved in the flesh and bones and sinews of those who live a celestial law, which is the law of the gospel. It is there to be read by others, first, by those who, seeing the good works of the Saints, shall respond by glorifying our Father in heaven, and finally by the Great Judge to whom every man's life is an open book."[7]

The body of Christ—the church of Jesus Christ—is made up of more than people who look nice or even who act nice. The church is composed of more than visibly obedient people, more than individuals who are ostensibly observant in their behavior. The followers of the Nazarene seek to be what they preach, to embody what they proclaim. They thereby make a difference in a world which so desperately needs them.

NOTES

1. Ralph Gower, *The New Manners and Customs of Bible Times* (Chicago: Moody Press, 1987), p. 53.
2. Gower, *Manners and Customs of Bible Times*, pp. 244–45.
3. *The Cost of Discipleship*, rev. ed. (New York: Macmillan, 1963), p. 129.
4. In Conference Report, Apr. 1980, p. 60; emphasis added.
5. Gower, *Manners and Customs of Bible Times*, p. 56.
6. In Conference Report, Apr. 1980, p. 60; emphasis in original.
7. In Conference Report, Oct. 1968, p. 135.

Chapter 9

THE LIGHT OF THE WORLD

The Lord calls us to point the way. In a world which is too often shrouded in uncertainty and doubt, the Light of Life bids us to let our light shine, to stand as beacons in the storms of the night, and to certify our discipleship by preachment and practice. Discipleship entails example. Discipleship involves standing out from the generality of mankind and standing up for what is true and right and good. We come to make a difference only when we are different, and that difference must be substantive enough to be witnessed and then acknowledged by others.

The scriptures repeatedly declare that Jesus Christ came into the world, that the Light shone in a world of darkness, and the darkness comprehended it not (John 1:5; D&C 34:2; 88:49). In one sense, that which was dark could not understand, could not grasp or perceive, that which was Light, for darkness is antithetical to light. Jesus was of all men and women most misunderstood. In another sense, darkness—the world of evil—could not conquer, could not overpower or control, that which was Light, for Jesus was and is the Lord of all—the Lord of light and darkness. His disciples will never really be understood by those who walk in the shadows. And his disciples must not, if they are to shine forth into the gloom of an apostate and hungry world, allow their light to be quenched or their influence for good to be threatened.

"Verily, verily, I say unto you," the Christ implored in his sermon on the Mount, "I give unto you to be the light of the world; a city that is set on a hill cannot be hid" (JST, Matt. 5:16). Jesus calls us to be the source of example and of edification. President Harold B. Lee warned that "any Latter-day Saint in Church circles, in military service, in social life, or in the business community is looked upon not just as an individual, but as the visible Church today. Someone has said: 'Be careful how you act, because you may be the only Standard Church Works some people may ever read.' "[1] That is neither unfair nor unexpected. Perfect we may not be, but different we must always be.

In a world in which values and direction are set by consensus, the Savior bids his disciples to cleanse the inner vessel within themselves, work in harmony with others of the household of faith, and seek to build up and establish the cause of Zion. Zion, the society of the pure in heart, is a city of light. It stands in marked contrast to Babylon, the abode of darkness, the gathering place of the worldly and the wayward. Babylon is the city of man; Zion, the city of God. Zion is the receptacle of virtue; Babylon, the embodiment of vice. Babylon judges according to ephemeral whims and current trends; Zion, according to the rock of revealed religion. Zion thus becomes the banner, the ensign to which the honest in heart rally when they have become weary of the shifting sands of secularity. "Behold, I, the Lord, have made my church in these last days like unto a judge sitting on a hill, or in a high place, to judge the nations. For it shall come to pass that the inhabitants of Zion shall judge all things pertaining to Zion" (D&C 64:37–38).

Just as Jesus beckons his people to be the salt of the earth — to be willing and able to flavor, heal, and preserve the world — so he insists that they stand as a light to the world. He demands that they make a difference. And it is only as the light of truth burns within them, only as the light of the gospel shines forth from them, that darkness can be penetrated. "You cannot lift another soul," President Lee instructed the Saints, "until you are standing on higher ground than he is. You must be sure, if you would rescue the man, that you yourself are setting the example of what you would have him be. *You cannot light a fire in another soul unless it is burning in your own soul.*"[2]

In one sense, the disciples of Christ place their candles, or lamps, under a bushel basket whenever they are not true to the light they have been given. For example, the Latter-day Saints in Kirtland received a divine mandate to construct a temple to their God. They failed to move forward to fulfill this commandment in a manner that pleased the Lord. A revelation thus explained that "there are many who have been ordained among you, whom I have called but few of them are chosen. They who are not chosen have sinned a very grievous sin, in that they are walking in darkness at noon day" (D&C 95:5–6). Similarly, the Lord had explained some months earlier—and modern prophets have emphasized the same in our own time—that because of our having treated lightly the Book of Mormon and modern revelation, our minds have been darkened; a condemnation, scourge, and judgment rest upon all the children of Zion. The way of deliverance is clear: "I will forgive you of your sins with this commandment—that you remain steadfast in your minds in solemnity and the spirit of prayer, *in bearing testimony* to all the world of those things which are communicated unto you" (D&C 84:54–61; emphasis added). In short, we walk in darkness or hide our light whenever we fail to live up to our spiritual privileges.

In holding up the light of the gospel, we must never allow our eyes to wander. Nor must we forget who is the Source of the light. To do so is to risk the onslaught of pride and the smugness of self-security. Those who become overly impressed with themselves come to "read by the lamp of their own conceit" and, as a law unto themselves, come to "interpret by rules of their own contriving."[3] No, we must never permit our gaze to wander far afield. "Therefore, let your light so shine before this world, that they may see your good works, *and glorify your Father who is in heaven*" (JST, Matt. 5:18; emphasis added). We allow our light to shine—our testimonies, our witness of the truthfulness of the work in which we are engaged, and our deeds of

49

Christian service — not that observers might commend and praise us but that they might turn their lives toward him who is the source of conviction and the personification of goodness. "Therefore, hold up your light that it may shine unto the world. Behold I am the light which ye should hold up — that which ye have seen me do" (3 Ne. 18:24). Christ is the Light. We are at best lamps, dim reflections of him. But to the degree that the light of his Spirit shines in our souls, to the degree that his image is in our countenances, to the degree that our good works motivate others to sing the song of redeeming love and glorify God, we are in the line of our duty as disciples.

Truly, the Lord is our light. As we bask in that which emanates from him, we prepare ourselves to go where his glorious light shall shine everlastingly. In speaking of the holy city, the celestialized earth, John said: "The city had no need of the sun, neither of the moon, to shine in it: for the glory of God did lighten it, and the Lamb is the light thereof. . . . And [the inhabitants of the city] shall see his face; and his name shall be in their foreheads. And there shall be no night there; and they need no candle, neither light of the sun; for the Lord God giveth them light: and they shall reign for ever and ever" (Rev. 21:23; 22:4–5).

NOTES

1. *Ye Are the Light of the World* (Salt Lake City: Deseret Book, 1974), p. 13.

2. In Conference Report, Apr. 1973, p. 178; emphasis added.

3. Joseph F. Smith, *Gospel Doctrine* (Salt Lake City: Deseret Book Co., 1971), p. 373.

Chapter 10

IF THY RIGHT EYE OFFEND THEE

To come unto Christ is to forsake the carnal world. It is to put away from us all that defiles or detracts or deters. To the children of Israel in the days of Moses, Jehovah said, "Ye shall be unto me a kingdom of priests, and an holy nation" (Exo. 19:6). Indeed, since the beginning the Lord has sought to make of the people of earth "a chosen generation, a royal priesthood, an holy nation, a peculiar people," sons and daughters who would "shew forth the praises of him who hath called [them] out of darkness into his marvellous light" (1 Pet. 2:9). In order to be holy, however, the Saints were and are required to separate themselves from the ways of the world. "Go ye out from among the wicked. Save yourselves" (D&C 38:42), the Almighty pleads. That is, "Go ye out from Babylon. Be ye clean that bear the vessels of the Lord" (D&C 133:5).

Anciently, those responsible for the handling and upkeep of sacred things, such as the Levites who assisted the priests in temple services, were expected to sanctify themselves, to see to it that they had clean hands and a pure heart. In our day, those who bear the priesthood, who, for example, attend to the sacrament, administer to the sick, baptize or confirm, labor in behalf of the living and the dead in holy temples — all such surely "bear the vessels of the Lord" and are expected to live in a manner that would in no way block or impede the flow of the Spirit of the Lord to those in whose behalf they minister. In addition, those who have received the witness of the Spirit as to the

51

truthfulness of this great latter-day work, who have enjoyed the gifts and powers of the Holy Ghost, and who have the unspeakable blessing of having living prophets and apostles in their midst—these also are counseled to be careful how they receive that which is sacred.

"Therefore, thou art blessed from henceforth that bear the keys of the kingdom given unto you; which kingdom is coming forth for the last time.

"Verily I say unto you, the keys of this kingdom shall never be taken from you [Joseph Smith], while thou art in the world, neither in the world to come;

"Nevertheless, through you shall the oracles [revelations] be given to another, yea, even unto the church.

"And *all they who receive the oracles of God, let them beware how they hold them lest they are accounted as a light thing, and are brought under condemnation thereby,* and stumble and fall when the storms descend, and the winds blow, and the rains descend, and beat upon their house" (D&C 90:2–5; emphasis added).

In the Sermon on the Mount, Jesus taught that "if thy right eye offend thee, pluck it out and cast it from thee; for it is profitable for thee that one of thy members should perish, and not that thy whole body should be cast into hell. Or if thy right hand offend thee, cut it off and cast it from thee; for it is profitable for thee that one of thy members should perish, and not that thy whole body should be cast into hell." And then the Savior explained himself: "And now *this I speak, a parable concerning your sins; wherefore, cast them from you, that ye may not be hewn down and cast into the fire*" (JST, Matt. 5:32–34; emphasis added). Later the Master reemphasized this principle when he said: "If thy hand or thy foot offend thee, cut it off and cast it from thee; for it is better for thee to enter into life halt or maimed, rather than having two hands or two feet to be cast into everlasting fire. And if thine eye offend thee, pluck it out and cast it from thee. . . . And *a man's hand is his friend, and his foot, also; and a man's eye, are they of his own household*" (JST, Matt. 18:7–9; emphasis added).

In a literal sense, we would be better off not having a mouth than having one that uttered blasphemies, or bore false witness, or was a degrading influence to others. It would be better not to have feet that are swift to run to mischief or hands that shed innocent blood. But the Lord of Life is speaking not in literal terms but in metaphoric terms of the need to rid ourselves of the elements in our personality or our associations that might dilute our discipleship. Just as it is excruciatingly painful to pluck out an eye, so it is painful to excise sin from our souls. Just as having a hand or a foot cut off is terrible agony, so also is it extremely difficult to sever those associations that hinder more than help. If in the process of attempting to help lift one another's burdens, we find ourselves burdened by the same sins or difficulties, we need to lift ourselves out of the situation. It is one thing to be a second-miler and quite another to accompany someone down the broad road to destruction.

In the Prophet Joseph Smith's inspired translation of Mark's Gospel, we find the Savior's explanation of this requirement of discipleship elucidated even more. Here we see that institutionally (as a Church), as well as individually, it is necessary to maintain the sanctity of the temple of God and for individual members to be guided and safeguarded by a personal witness and commitment.

"Therefore, if thy hand offend thee, cut it off; or *if thy brother offend thee and confess not and forsake not, he shall be cut off.* It is better for thee to enter into life maimed, than having two hands, to go into hell.

"For it is better for thee to enter into life without thy brother, than for thee and thy brother to be cast into hell; into the fire that never shall be quenched, where their worm [torment, agony] dieth not, and the fire is not quenched.

"And again, if thy foot offend thee, cut it off; for *he that is thy standard, by whom thou walkest, if he become a transgressor, he shall be cut off.*

"It is better for thee, to enter halt into life, than having two feet to be cast into hell; into the fire that never shall be quenched.

"Therefore, *let every man stand or fall, by himself, and not for another; or not trusting another*" (JST, Mark 9:40–44; emphasis added).

Truly, "it is upon the rock of our Redeemer, who is Christ, the Son of God, that ye must build your foundation; that when the devil shall send forth his mighty winds, yea, his shafts in the whirlwind, yea, when all his hail and his mighty storm shall beat upon you, it shall have no power over you to drag you down to the gulf of misery and endless wo, because of the rock upon which ye are built, which is a sure foundation, a foundation whereon if men build they cannot fall" (Hel. 5:12).

Disciples are called to walk and live a disciplined way of life. Theirs is not a sterile asceticism, nor a rigidness and inflexibility born of fanaticism. Rather, their task is to seek to remain aloof from the elements of a fallen world that loosen our hold on eternal verities. As a Christian soldier, he clothes himself in "the whole armor of God" (Eph. 6:11–18; D&C 27:15–18); she learns to "touch not the unclean thing" (2 Cor. 6:14). In our day the Lord spoke: "Behold, I, the Lord, who was crucified for the sins of the world, give unto you a commandment that you shall forsake the world" (D&C 53:2). Disciples live in the world. They seek to better the world by their presence, but they also seek the rewards of a better world.

Chapter 11

LET NOT THE
LEFT HAND KNOW

The call to discipleship is a call to a higher righteousness. The Saints are asked to put off the natural man, put away the toys of a telestial world, and grow up in the Lord. They are summoned to be obedient, to keep the commandments, to manifest "by a godly walk and conversation that they are worthy" of membership in the Church and kingdom of God (D&C 20:69). They covenant to take upon them the sacred name of Jesus Christ, to bear the same with fidelity and devotion, and to behave as becomes Christians. In short, they covenant before God and man to see to it that their actions evidence their Christian commitment. Disciples are expected to have clean hands.

But there is more. Life in Christ is more than correct behavior, more than appropriate actions, more than what we *do*. It is being. It is what we *are*. True disciples seek that sanctifying influence that derives from the Holy Spirit, so that they come to do the right things for the right reasons. Life in Christ is characterized by pure attitudes, motives, and desires. Disciples are expected to have pure hearts. The Master thus taught:

"Verily, verily, I say that I would that ye should do alms [good deeds, service, assistance] unto the poor; but take heed that ye do not your alms before men to be seen of them; otherwise ye have no reward of your Father who is in heaven.

"Therefore, when ye shall do your alms do not sound a

trumpet before you, as will hypocrites do in the synagogues and in the streets, that they may have glory of men. Verily I say unto you, they have their reward.

"But when thou doest alms let not thy left hand know what thy right hand doeth;

"That thine alms may be in secret; and thy Father who seeth in secret, himself shall reward thee openly" (3 Ne. 13:1–4).

We might suppose that service of any kind has merit. There is, however, a spiritual motivation that impels us to righteous deeds, which sanctifies giver and receiver. When the doers of the deed are single in their intent; when the givers focus far more on the one to be assisted than on their own comfort or appearance; when the alm, the offering is made wholly for the blessing and good of the receiver, then permanent and lasting good is accomplished and those involved know that the Lord is pleased.

Service that is self-serving is something less than service. Though we may not be evil individuals, yet to do good to be seen or noticed or heard, is certainly less than noble and may be symptomatic of inner evil. For "God hath said a man being evil cannot do that which is good; for if he offereth a gift, or prayeth unto God, except he shall do it with real intent it profiteth him nothing. For behold, *it is not counted unto him for righteousness. For behold, . . . it is counted unto him the same as if he had retained the gift*" (Moro. 7:6–8; emphasis added). A person who does good to be seen of others already has, in the words of Christ, the reward: the praise or esteem of the observers. The unspoken part of the Master's poignant warning is essentially: "And let not such a person expect a reward hereafter!" In warning of the importance of pure motives, Elder Dallin H. Oaks has written: "Priestcraft is the sin committed by the combination of a good act—such as preaching or teaching the gospel—and a bad motive. The act may be good and visible, but the sin is in the motive. On earth, the wrong motive may be known only to the actor, but in heaven it is always known to God."[1]

In exhorting his followers to see to it that their motive for

56

religious observance — specifically public prayer — was noble and appropriate, Jesus said: "When thou prayest thou shalt not do as the hypocrites, for they love to pray, standing in the synagogues and in the corners of the streets, that they may be seen of men. Verily, I say unto you, they have their reward" (3 Ne. 13:5). It would seem that of all things, our pleadings and petitions to the Almighty should be free of sham or pretense, void of the desire to impress others. The prophet Zenos, as a part of a plain but powerful prayer to God, provides a touching example of communion with the Infinite:

"Thou art merciful, O God, for thou hast heard my prayer, even when I was in the wilderness; yea, thou wast merciful when I prayed concerning those who were mine enemies, and thou didst turn them to me.

"Yea, O God, and thou wast merciful unto me when I did cry unto thee in my field; when I did cry unto thee in my prayer, and thou didst hear me.

"And again, O God, when I did turn to my house thou didst hear me in my prayer.

"And when I did turn unto my closet, O Lord, and prayed unto thee, thou didst hear me.

"Yea, thou art merciful unto thy children when they cry unto thee, *to be heard of thee and not of men*, and thou wilt hear them" (Alma 33:4–8; emphasis added).

The Prophet Joseph Smith understood this principle clearly. His petitions were fervent, his motives pure, and the blessings of heaven thereby regular. Daniel Tyler, a young associate of the Prophet, recalled a particular occasion:

"At the time William Smith and others rebelled against the Prophet at Kirtland, I attended a meeting . . . where Joseph presided. Entering the school house a little before the meeting opened and gazing upon the man of God, I perceived sadness in his countenance and tears trickling down his cheeks. A few moments later a hymn was sung and he opened the meeting by prayer. Instead of facing the audience, however, he turned his back and bowed upon his knees, facing the wall. This, I suppose, was done to hide his sorrow and tears.

"I had heard men and women pray — especially the former — from the most ignorant, both as to letters and intellect, to the most learned and eloquent. But never until then had I heard a man address his Maker as though He was present listening as a kind father would listen to the sorrows of a dutiful child. Joseph was at that time unlearned, but that prayer, which was to a considerable extent in behalf of those who accused him of having gone astray and fallen into sin, was that the Lord would forgive them and open their eyes that they might see aright. *That prayer, I say, to my humble mind, partook of the learning and eloquence of heaven. There was no ostentation, no raising of the voice as by enthusiasm, but a plain conversational tone,* as a man would address a present friend. It appeared to me as though, in case the veil were taken away, I could see the Lord standing facing His humblest of all servants I had ever seen. It was the crowning of all the prayers I ever heard."[2]

Our prayers are to God, not to men. Our yearnings for divine assistance are addressed to the Man of Holiness, not to unholy and finite men and women. Too often, as the Savior taught, those who trust "in themselves that they [are] righteous" do not enjoy the peace and ratifying seal of the Lord's acceptance upon either their prayers or their performances (see Luke 18:9–14). The esteem and approbation of the present world cannot bestow those silent but certain honors that will come in the Savior's due time to the pure in heart.

What, then, is the duty of the developing disciple? What does a man or a woman do whose motives are not absolutely pure? In short, what of many of us who hold membership in the Church of Jesus Christ? Do we sit back and avoid deeds of service because our desires are not yet sanctified? Do we refrain from home or visiting teaching, for example, because our motivation is presently clouded more by the spirit of inspection than of expectation and covenant? Certainly not. We have duties to perform, work to do in order to bear off the kingdom of God triumphant. And Zion—as well as its municipals, its citizenry—is being established "in process of time" (Moses 7:21). Simply stated, disciples do not wait to be transformed before they proceed in the work of the ministry. Missionaries do not wait in their apartments for an outpouring of the Spirit before they approach the first door. Rather, they seek to purify themselves from sin, pray intently for divine direction and power, and then proceed confidently that the needed endowment will be forthcoming when the Lord sees fit to send it.

The quest for a pure heart is the quest for pure motives and desires. Surely one of the most significant requests disciples make of their Redeemer is for a cleansing and purifying of motives, a greater desire to do the right things for the right reason. To have a situation wherein the left hand does not know what the right hand is doing is to be in a condition where there is no ulterior motivation, no hidden agenda, no selfish purposes for our actions. In one sense, then, the challenge of disciples in this regard is to rise above self, above self-regard, above self-inspection. Dietrich Bonhoeffer, in addressing a paradox in the Sermon on the Mount—the command to "let your light so shine before men" (Matt. 5:16) versus the command to "take heed that ye do not your alms before men" (Matt. 6:1)—wrote:

"How is this paradox to be resolved? The first question to ask is: From whom are we to hide the visibility of our discipleship? Certainly not from other men, for we are told to let them see our light. No. *We are to hide it from ourselves.* Our task is simply to keep on following, looking only to our Leader who goes on before, *taking no notice of ourselves or of what we are doing. We must be unaware of our own righteousness,* and see it only insofar as we look unto Jesus; then it will seem not extraordinary, but quite ordinary and natural. . . . The Christian is a light unto the world, not because of any quality of his own, but only because he follows Christ and looks solely to him. . . .

"All that the follower of Jesus has to do is to make sure that his obedience, following and love are *entirely spontaneous and unpremeditated.* If you do good, you must not let your left hand know what your right hand is doing, you must be quite unconscious of it. Otherwise you are simply displaying your own virtue, and not that which has its source in Jesus Christ. Christ's virtue, the virtue of discipleship, can only be accomplished so long as you are entirely *unconscious* of what you are doing. The genuine work of love is always a hidden work. . . .

"Thus hiddenness has its counterpart in manifestation. For there is nothing hidden that shall not be revealed. For our God is a God unto whom all hearts are open, and from whom no secrets are hid. God will show us the hidden and make it visible. Manifestation is the appointed reward for hiddenness, and the only question is where we shall receive it and who will give it us. If we want publicity in the eyes of men we have our reward. In other words, it is immaterial whether the publicity we want is the grosser kind, which all can see, or the more subtle variety which we can only see ourselves. If the left hand knows what the right hand is doing, if we become conscious of our hidden virtue, we are forging our own reward, instead of that which God had intended to give us in his own good time."[3]

To repeat, we are never justified in doing the wrong thing or ignoring the work to be done simply because we are not properly motivated. Rather, the Saints are instructed again and again to seek the Spirit, to ask for, live for, and qualify for the gifts and fruits of the Spirit, which characterize the sons and daughters of Jesus Christ (see Gal. 6:22–23; D&C 46). As that Spirit begins to live in us, to remake us, we come to love the things we before hated and to hate the things we before loved. Because the Spirit is His Spirit, the works likewise become his works. "Ye are built upon my gospel; therefore ye shall call whatsoever things ye do call, in my name; therefore if ye call upon the Father, for the church, if it be in my name the Father will hear you; and if it so be that the church is built upon my gospel then will the Father show forth his own works in it" (3 Ne. 27:9–10). Our service thereby is centered in Christ, our eye single to his glory.

NOTES

1. *Pure in Heart* (Salt Lake City: Bookcraft, 1988), p. 16.

2. In Hyrum and Helen Mae Andrus, *They Knew the Prophet* (Salt Lake City: Bookcraft, 1974), pp. 51–52; emphasis added.

3. *The Cost of Discipleship*, rev. ed. (New York: Macmillan, 1963), pp. 176–78; emphasis added.

Chapter 12

REMEMBER THE
POOR AND THE NEEDY

Early in this dispensation the Lord delivered a profound truth in few words: "It is not given," he said, "that one man should possess that which is above another, wherefore the world lieth in sin" (D&C 49:20). More than any other record or literary work, the Book of Mormon is a harsh reminder of the potential perils of prosperity, the evils of inequality, and the sin and sadness of systems in society which divide the children of God according to their material means or their chances for learning. On the other hand, the Book of Mormon prophets are quick to point out the sublime social order that prevails when individuals acknowledge their blessings with humility before God, seek out and see to the needs of the less fortunate, and strive tirelessly to eradicate differences between people and nations. Disciples of Christ, like their Master, cannot rest while others suffer. "And remember in all things the poor and the needy," comes the reminder, "the sick and the afflicted, for he that doeth not these things, the same is not my disciple" (D&C 52:40).

The care of the poor is a sign that the Spirit of the Lord is working among the Saints of God. About ninety years before the birth of Jesus Christ, a tremendous polarizing took place among the people of Nephi between those who were committed to the work of the Church and those who were not. Great numbers left the gospel path because of the hardness of their hearts, while others remained true and faithful to their trusts and enjoyed the sweet fruits of life in Christ. Mormon records:

"And they did impart of their substance, every man according to that which he had, to the poor, and the needy, and the sick, and the afflicted; and they did not wear costly apparel, yet they were neat and comely.

"And thus they did establish the affairs of the church; and thus they began to have continual peace again, notwithstanding all their persecutions.

"And now, because of the steadiness of the church they began to be exceedingly rich, having abundance of all things whatsoever they stood in need. . . .

"And thus, in their prosperous circumstances, they did not send away any who were naked, or that were hungry, or that were athirst, or that were sick, or that had not been nourished; and they did not set their hearts upon riches; therefore they were liberal to all, both old and young, both bond and free, both male and female, whether out of the church or in the church, having no respect to persons as to those who stood in need" (Alma 1:27–30).

The care of the poor is more than a duty, far more than a Christian obligation. It is a royal opportunity to live the "royal law," namely, "Thou shalt love thy neighbour as thyself" (James 2:8). As we have suggested earlier, when such is undertaken in the true spirit of fellowship, both giver and receiver are sanctified by the effort. King Benjamin taught his people that after a person has obtained a remission of sins, that the key to *retaining* that justified state from day to day is to care for the poor. Note his words: "And now, for the sake of . . . retaining a remission of your sins from day to day, that ye may walk guiltless before God—I would that ye should impart of your substance to the poor, every man according to that which he hath, such as feeding the hungry, clothing the naked, visiting the sick and administering to their relief, both spiritually and temporally, according to their wants" (Mosiah 4:26).

No person walks the path of life blameless. Jesus only was perfect, in the sense that he committed no sin and took no detours. But the Lord promises his disciples that if they will look to the needs of others and offer themselves willingly as under-shepherds—seeking at the same time with all their hearts to remain free from the taints of the world—he will remit their sins, pronounce them innocent at the last day, and welcome them into his presence. We are told, for example, that those who embark in the service of God, and who do so with all their heart, might, mind, and strength—we are told that they shall stand blameless before God at the last day (D&C 4:1–2). It is not that such persons would never have committed sin, or even that they would have been so busy in doing good that they were unable to do so. Rather, as an act of his mercy and grace, in combination with the good works and deeds of his disciples, the Savior justifies them, exonerates them from their misdeeds.

In a modern revelation we learn that Jesus did not receive of the fulness of the glory of his Father at the first but progressed line upon line, grace for grace, and from grace to grace. That is, he received additional strength and power from the Father as he gave himself in service to his fellowmen (grace *for* grace). Further, he developed from one spiritual level to a greater, until in the resurrection he gained the fulness (from grace *to* grace). After having described his own pathway to godhood, the Lord declared: "I give unto you these sayings that you may understand and know how to worship, and know what you worship, that you may come unto the Father in my name, and in due time receive of his fulness. For if you keep my commandments you shall receive of his fulness, and be glorified in me as I am in the Father; therefore, I say unto you, you shall receive grace for grace" (D&C 93:19–20). We learn from this passage that the essence of true worship of our Savior is emulation, imitation of the deeds he performed, of his charitable service in behalf of our brothers and sisters. In this sense, we worship him as we serve and care for them. We come to the Father and grow in spiritual graces just as he did—through service. Indeed, charity prevents a multitude of sins (1 Pet. 4:8).

And yet, given that there are millions of hungry and naked and destitute souls in the world, how are disciples to live with themselves? How are we to handle the fact that there is only so much we can do, only so many we can assist and still manage to care for our own? King Benjamin advised wisely that "all these things"—our efforts to care for the needy—must be "done in wisdom and order; for it is not requisite that a man should run faster than he has strength. And again, it is expedient that he should be diligent, that thereby he might win the prize; therefore, all things must be done in order" (Mosiah 4:27). If every family contributed regularly to every needy cause, there would be insufficient money for the family to live. If every Christian man or woman gave themselves consistently to every project designed to alleviate suffering, there would be no time to earn a living or care for their own. True disciples pray for discernment and for discretion. They seek to be as generous and giving as is appropriate and practical. To begin with, they pay their tithes and contribute generously to the fast offerings of the Church. They visit and care and pray for those assigned to their care. And they are sensitive to friends and neighbors—within or without the Church—who are in need. Beyond that, Christians seek to do what they can, knowing, as Benjamin taught, that we are all beggars before the Lord. Disciples who honestly cannot contribute say in their heart: "I give not because I have not, but if I had I would give" (Mosiah 4:19–20, 24). Even when we are not in a position to contribute dramatically to the alleviation of hunger in Africa or India, for example, there is still something we can do, something vital for those who aspire to discipleship. We can avoid as we would a plague the tendency to be indifferent, to ignore the problem because it is not in our own backyards. Further, we can teach our families or friends by precept and by example to use wisely the food and other resources we have been blessed to have. Even if we just become aware of suffering and pain, our heightened sensitivity helps us deal more tenderly, more charitably, with sufferers within our own limited reach. At least those are starting points.

Anciently the Lord "called his people Zion, because they were of one heart and one mind, and dwelt in righteousness;

and there was no poor among them" (Moses 7:18). We remember that King Benjamin directed his people to care for the needs of the poor, both temporally and spiritually. Not all of those who are poor are financially insolvent. Some are poor spiritually, heavy with sin. Some are poor emotionally, burdened down with the cares of family or distraught over personal struggles or broken relationships. The disciple of Christ is called upon to be aware and attuned to such needs. "The greatest miracles I see today," President Harold B. Lee stated, "are not necessarily the healing of sick bodies, but the greatest miracles I see are the healing of sick souls, those who are sick in soul and spirit and are downhearted and distraught, on the verge of nervous break-downs. We are reaching out to all such, because they are precious in the sight of the Lord, and we want no one to feel that they are forgotten."[1] The disciple of Christ longs and labors for the day when all will be converted fully to the Lord; when no contentions or disputations exist to divide and scar the spirit; when men and women — made free and partakers of the heavenly gift — deal justly with one another, all because of the love of God which exists in the hearts of the people (see 4 Ne. 1:1–16). In that day Zion will be redeemed and the earth shall rest.

NOTE

1. In Conference Report, Apr. 1973, p. 178.

Chapter 13

IF YE HAVE LOVE
ONE TO ANOTHER

One dramatic evidence of apostasy in the world today is a growing sense of indifference toward and among the sons and daughters of God. Man's inhumanity to man is one of the signs of the times, the fulfillment of prophecy. "Because iniquity shall abound," the Savior taught before his death, "the love of men shall wax cold" (JS–H 1:30; compare D&C 45:27). "It is one evidence," Joseph Smith the Prophet explained, "that men are unacquainted with the principles of godliness to behold the contraction of affectionate feelings and lack of charity in the world." On the other hand, those who come unto Christ become as Christ. They partake of his divine nature, receive his attributes, and come to love as he loves. "The nearer we get to our heavenly Father," the modern seer went on to say, "the more we are disposed to look with compassion on perishing souls; we feel that we want to take them upon our shoulders, and cast their sins behind our backs."[1] Disciples of Christ seek to acquire the love of Christ, for "love is one of the chief characteristics of Deity, and ought to be manifested by those who aspire to be the sons of God."[2]

At the Last Supper, our Savior—surely heavy with anticipation in regard to the coming crisis in Gethsemane—sought to unite the Twelve. He taught them pure doctrine. He focused on matters of substance. He pleaded with them (and with the Father in their behalf) to be one. He said: "A new commandment I give unto you, That ye love one another; as I have loved you, that ye also love one another." A *new* commandment? Had not Jesus taught them to love before? Had not Jehovah spoken of this transcendent truth over the millennia? A new commandment? Certainly not new in the sense that it was being introduced for the first time. In the words of Elder Bruce R. McConkie, the Lord "desired to emphasize anew the eternal importance of the law of love."

"Whenever the Lord has given the fulness of his gospel to any people, from the day of Adam to the present hour, it has always included the command that his saints love one another. Even under the law of Moses, the divine command was, 'thou shalt love thy neighbour as thyself' (Lev. 19:18), and Jesus himself had gone so far as to say, 'Love your enemies' (Matt. 5:44). And yet when he later brought forward the law of love, giving it an entirely new emphasis and force, his words were, 'A new commandment I give unto you, That ye love one another' (John 13:34).

"There was nothing new about this law of love except that it was being restated anew; it was coming again—newly, as it were—to disciples of whom it had been expected all along."[3]

John the Apostle later wrote a message that was in harmony with what had been given him: "Brethren, I write a new commandment unto you, but it is the same commandment which ye had from the beginning. The old commandment is the word which ye have heard from the beginning. Again, a new commandment I write unto you, which thing was of old ordained of God; and is true in him, and in you: because the darkness is past, and the true light now shineth" (JST, 1 Jn. 2:7–8). "By this shall all men know that ye are my disciples, if ye have love one to another" (John 13:35).

Charity is the "pure love of Christ" (Moro. 7:47). To have charity is to love Christ purely and to love purely, just as Christ does. These two are certainly not unrelated, and, to some degree, we love and serve others more naturally when we love and honor the Lord. In the first sense, to have charity is to feel a profound sense of love for the Lord, to be eager to acknowledge his hand in all things, to "sing the song of redeeming love" (Alma 5:14). President George F. Richards spoke once of having seen Christ in a dream: "He spoke no word to me, but my love for him was such that I have not words to explain. I know that no mortal man can love the Lord as I experienced that love for the Savior unless God reveals it to him."[4] Thus, as President Ezra Taft Benson observed, "To love God with all your heart, soul, mind, and strength is all-consuming and all encompassing. . . . The breadth, depth, and height of this love of God extend into every facet of one's life. Our desires, be they spiritual or temporal, should be rooted in a love of the Lord."[5] Ethical deeds, works of faith, acts of kindness towards others—these are so much more effective and pure when grounded in the love of Deity.

It goes without saying that disciples of Christ ought to love one another. They have in common those things that matter most in life. Their view of reality ("things as they really are"—Jacob 4:13), their goals and ambitions, their hopes and dreams for here and hereafter—all these things they share with members of the Church far and wide. They are bonded together, clothed in the bond of charity, that mantle "which is the bond of perfectness and peace" (D&C 88:125). Disciples of Christ enjoy the gift that is the greatest gift available to men and women in mortality—the gift of the Holy Ghost. Love, or charity, is a gift of the Spirit, and those who cultivate that Spirit receive from time to time that heavenly endowment Mormon described as "the pure love of Christ."

The expression of the love of God is not to be limited, however, to the household of faith (D&C 121:45). We have a duty beyond the fold as well, and the Spirit, which is the source of pure love, expands our vision to see and feel as we ought. Joseph Smith taught: "There is a love from God that should be exercised toward those of our faith, who walk uprightly, which is peculiar to itself, but it is without prejudice; it also gives scope to the mind, which enables us to conduct ourselves with greater liberality towards all that are not of our faith, than what they exercise towards one another. These principles approximate

69

nearer to the mind of God, because it is like God, or Godlike."[6] "A man filled with the love of God," the Prophet said on a later occasion, "is not content with blessing his family alone, but ranges through the whole world, anxious to bless the whole human race."[7] President Ezra Taft Benson has taught that "we must develop a love for people. Our hearts must go out to them in the pure love of the gospel, in a desire to lift them, to build them up, to point them to a higher, finer, life and eventually to exaltation in the celestial kingdom of God."[8]

Service is absolutely essential if we desire to follow our Lord and Master. But that service is lasting and life-changing when it is motivated by pure love. Charity is something which must be bestowed from above; it is a gift, one which must be sought and acquired by spiritual means. "Wherefore, my beloved brethren," Mormon implored, "pray unto the Father with all the energy of heart, that ye may be filled with this love, which he hath bestowed upon all who are true followers of his Son, Jesus Christ; that ye may become the sons of God; that when he shall appear we shall be like him, for we shall see him as he is; that we may have this hope; that we may be purified even as he is pure" (Moro. 7:48). It will not be sufficient to be *with* the Lord when he comes; the disciple desires to be *like* him. We will not only be righteous as he is; we will love as he does. The scope and sweeping perspective that charity grants, the spirit of liberality toward all, will have consumed and transformed the people of God, such that they feel humble but confident to dwell with him.

In a world that has lost its focus, in a time when men and women refuse to bridle their passions and thus revoke the powers of godliness within them, in an age when angst and hopelessness cloud the vision of so many, the Savior and Prince of Peace offers relief. Were it not for the promises and precious gifts of God, we might fear and despair. But we need not be startled by what man can do, for perfect love casts out fear (Moro. 8:16; 1 Jn. 4:8)—fear of failure, fear of rejection, fear of finding ourselves. The path of the disciple is the path of peace, the path of hope, the path of rest. Mormon wrote to the Saints of his day: "Wherefore, I would speak unto you that are of the church, that are the peaceable followers of Christ, and that have obtained a sufficient hope by which ye can enter into the rest of the Lord, from this time henceforth until ye shall rest with him in heaven" (Moro. 7:3). The peaceable followers of Christ, filled with love for God and man, have entered into the rest of the Lord; they possess "a settled conviction of the truth." Entering the rest of the Lord in this life consists of "entering the knowledge and love of God, having faith in his purpose and in his plan." This state is a rest "from doubt, from fear, from apprehension of danger, rest from the religious turmoil of the world."[9]

Mormon explained that "the remission of sins bringeth meekness, and lowliness of heart; and because of meekness and lowliness of heart cometh the visitation of the Holy Ghost, which Comforter filleth with hope and perfect love, which love endureth by diligence unto prayer, until the end shall come, when all the saints shall dwell with God" (Moro. 8:26). The disciple who enters the rest of the Lord in this life is preparing for the glorious rest to come hereafter, the fulness of the glory of God (D&C 84:24). Alma thus encouraged the people of Ammonihah to "be led by the Holy Spirit, becoming humble, meek, submissive, patient, full of love and all long-suffering; having faith on the Lord; having a hope that ye shall receive eternal life; having the love of God always in your hearts, that ye may be lifted up at the last day and enter into his rest" (Alma 13:28–29). That is perhaps related to what the Prophet Joseph Smith meant when he spoke of the spiritual safeguard of possessing charity: "Many of us have gone at the command of the Lord in defiance of everything evil," he said, "and obtained blessings unspeakable, in consequence of which our names are sealed in the Lamb's book of life, for the Lord has spoken it." Then he added: "Until we have perfect love we are liable to fall and when we have a testimony that our names are sealed in the Lamb's book of life we have perfect love and then it is impossible for false Christs to deceive us."[10]

Love is the process. Love is the product. It is the heart and core of discipleship.

NOTES

1. *Teachings of the Prophet Joseph Smith,* sel. Joseph Fielding Smith (Salt Lake City: Deseret Book Co., 1976), pp. 240–41.

2. *Teachings of the Prophet Joseph Smith,* p. 174.

3. *Ensign,* Aug. 1976, p. 8.

4. Cited by Spencer W. Kimball, in Conference Report, Apr. 1974, pp. 173–74.

5. *Teachings of Ezra Taft Benson* (Salt Lake City: Bookcraft, 1988), p. 349.

6. *Teachings of the Prophet Joseph Smith,* p. 147.

7. *Teachings of the Prophet Joseph Smith,* p. 174.

8. *Come unto Christ* (Salt Lake City: Deseret Book Co., 1983), p. 96.

9. Joseph F. Smith, *Gospel Doctrine* (Salt Lake City: Deseret Book Co., 1971), pp. 126, 58.

10. *Teachings of the Prophet Joseph Smith,* p. 9.

Chapter 14

OUT OF SMALL THINGS

The lengthy trek to Zion is accomplished one step at a time. Just as we do not generally bound into the celestial kingdom after only a brief mortal experience and testing, so also we do not qualify to be called a disciple of Christ by monumental moves alone. Though in the overall scheme of things, once in a great while we as Christians may be called upon to lay down our lives in the cause of truth, far more often we are expected to live our religion daily, to perform those quiet and simple acts that over a lifetime forge an eternal character. The giant leap to godhood is undertaken by one small step at a time.

"We observe vast, sweeping world events," Elder M. Russell Ballard remarked; "however, we must remember that the purposes of the Lord in our personal lives generally are fulfilled through the small and simple things, and not the momentous and spectacular."[1] That was a lesson Alma sought to teach to his son Helaman. In emphasizing the importance of the plates of brass in the dealings of the Nephites, Alma remarked that "they should be kept and handed down from one generation to another, and be kept and preserved by the hand of the Lord until they should go forth unto every nation, kindred, tongue, and people, that they shall know of the mysteries contained therein." It may be that Alma then focused upon the matter of simply taking good care of these records, for he said: "And now behold, if they are kept they must retain their brightness; yea, and they will retain their brightness; yea, and also shall all the plates which do contain that which is holy writ." Whether the word *brightness* refers to their spiritual significance or to their physical condition—being free from tarnish and corrosion, for example—we cannot tell. But in principle, at least, the latter meaning certainly has application here. "Now ye may suppose that this is foolishness in me; but behold I say unto you, that by small and simple things are great things brought to pass; and small means in many instances doth confound the wise. And the Lord God doth work by means to bring about his great and eternal purposes; and by very small means the Lord doth confound the wise and bringeth about the salvation of many souls" (Alma 37:4–7). It is as though Alma were saying: "It may not seem too significant at this point, but the physical upkeep of these records—what may seem small to some—is vital. They have been preserved in order to be read and studied, and their influence will thus be great."

Later in the same chapter Alma directed Helaman's attention to another matter—the Liahona, or compass, given by God to Lehi—to reinforce that underlying lesson. "There cannot any man work after the manner of so curious [skillful] a workmanship. And behold, it was prepared to show unto our fathers the course which they should travel in the wilderness. And it did work for them according to their faith in God . . . therefore they had this miracle, and also many other miracles wrought by the power of God, day by day." Thus the miraculous was brought to pass through the simple exercise of faith. "Nevertheless, because those miracles were worked by small means it did show unto them marvelous works." Alma then counseled Helaman to exercise simple faith in God, give heed to the words of Christ, that the people might eventually inherit "a far better land of promise," the celestial kingdom (Alma 37:38–45).

The principle that great things flow from small things was likewise taught by Nephi centuries earlier in regard to the Liahona: "I, Nephi, beheld the pointers which were in the ball, that they did work according to the faith and diligence and heed which we did give unto them. And there was also written upon them a new writing, which was plain to be read, which did give us understanding concerning the ways of the Lord; and it was written and changed from time to time, according to the faith and diligence which we gave unto it. And thus we see that by small means the Lord can bring about great things" (1 Ne. 16:28–29).

Disciples are not obsessed with the marvelous and mountain-moving works to be done; rather, they concentrate upon the task at hand, resting assured that small steps contribute eventually to the realization of the great. An experience from the Old Testament illustrates this principle beautifully. Naaman, a Syrian military leader and a good man, was stricken with leprosy. A young Israelite maid, a servant of Naaman's wife, knew of her master's condition. She also knew that deliverance from his horrid condition was possible. "She said unto her mistress, Would God my lord were with the prophet [Elisha] that is in Samaria! for he would recover him of the leprosy." Naaman finally came "with his horses and with his chariot, and stood at the door of the house of Elisha. And Elisha sent a messenger unto him, saying, Go and wash in [the Jordan River] seven times, and thy flesh shall come again to thee, and thou shalt be clean." Naaman's pride was wounded on two counts. First, why couldn't Elisha take the time to come out of the house, meet him, and then heal him by the laying on of hands? Second, Naaman reasoned: What is it about the Jordan River? Why that filthy place? "Are not Arbana and Pharpar, rivers of Damascus, better than all the waters of Israel? may I not wash in them, and be clean? So he turned and went away in a rage." And then the timeless lesson. The sensitive servants of Naaman asked the question of the ages: "If the prophet had bid thee do some great thing, wouldest thou not have done it? how much rather then, when he saith to thee, Wash and be clean?" No doubt convicted by the poignance and spirit of truthfulness in their words, Naaman humbled himself. "Then he went down, and dipped himself seven times in Jordan, according to the saying of the man of

God: and his flesh came again like unto the flesh of a little child, and he was clean" (2 Kgs. 5:1–14).

Well might we ask: If the Prophet Joseph had asked me to journey to Missouri, would I have gone? If the Lord had called me to serve as an apostle, would I have accepted? If I were asked to tend the children or grandchildren of the members of the First Presidency, would I hesitate? If I had been bidden to attend the School of the Prophets, would I take along my scriptures, study and prepare ahead of time, and attend regularly? If my call to serve as a home or visiting teacher had come to me through an open vision, would I accept? Would I be faithful? "You can put it down in your little black book," Elder Boyd K. Packer has warned us, "that *if you will not be loyal in the small things, you will not be loyal in the large things.* If you will not respond to the so-called insignificant or menial tasks which need to be performed in the Church and Kingdom, there will be no opportunity for service in the so-called greater challenges. A man who says he will sustain the President of the Church or the General Authorities, but cannot sustain his own bishop, is deceiving himself. The man who will not sustain the bishop of his ward and the president of his stake will not sustain the President of the Church."[2]

"A series of seemingly small but incorrect choices," Elder M. Russell Ballard pointed out, "can become those little soul-destroying termites that eat away at the foundations of our testimony until, before we are aware, we may be brought near to spiritual and moral destruction."[3] In a similar way, the small acts of kindness, the tiny deeds of Christian service, the silent but significant efforts to control our own thoughts and feelings — these are the simple things that build character and shape human destiny everlastingly. The world takes notice of the public accomplishments, the spectacular victories. But who knows of the private battles of the soul, thousands of them, waged and won by Abraham long before he passed his greatest test on Mount Moriah to become the friend of God? Who knows of the infinite struggles, the buffetings, the adversarial onslaughts faced and overcome by the sinless Son of Man in the Garden of the Oilpress, finished before his public victory over the grave on Golgotha? Truly, the "little things" form and shape the disciple of Christ.

President Joseph F. Smith offered an insight into the significance of the small things. "After all," he said, "to do well those things which God ordained to be the common lot of all mankind, is the truest greatness.

"To be a successful father or a successful mother is greater than to be a successful general or a successful statesman. One is universal and eternal greatness; the other is ephemeral. It is true that such secondary greatness may be added to that which we style commonplace; but when such secondary greatness is not added to that which is fundamental, it is merely an empty honor, and fades away from the common and universal good in life, even though it may find a place in the desultory pages of history. Our first care, after all, brings us back to that beautiful admonition of our Savior: 'Seek ye first the kingdom of God, and his righteousness; and all these things shall be added unto you' (Matt. 6:33).

"*We should never be discouraged in those daily tasks which God has ordained to the common lot of man.* Each day's labor should be undertaken in a joyous spirit and with the thought and conviction that our happiness and eternal welfare depend upon doing well that which we ought to do, that which God has made it our duty to do. Many are unhappy because they imagine that they should be doing something unusual or something phenomenal. Some people would rather be the blossom of a tree and be admiringly seen than be an enduring part of the tree and live the commonplace life of the tree's existence.

"Let us not be trying," President Smith concluded, "to substitute an artificial life for the true one. He is truly happy who can see and appreciate the beauty with which God has adorned the commonplace things of life."[4]

Christian disciples seek for and obtain perspective on life. Disciples come to know that despite present difficulties or current challenges, eternal life comes to those who proceed along the strait and narrow in unspectacular but steady fashion. "Where-fore, be not weary in well-doing, for ye are laying the foundation of a great work. And out of small things proceedeth that which is great. Behold, the Lord requireth the heart and a willing mind; and the willing and obedient shall eat the good of the land of Zion in these last days" (D&C 64:33–34).

NOTES

1. *Ensign,* May 1990, p. 6.
2. "Follow the Brethren," *Speeches of the Year* (Provo, Utah: Brigham Young University Press, 1965), pp. 4–5; emphasis added.
3. *Ensign,* May 1990, p. 7.
4. *Gospel Doctrine* (Salt Lake City: Deseret Book Co., 1971), pp. 285–86; emphasis added.

Chapter 15

IF YE CONTINUE IN MY WORD

The disciple is called to proceed along the strait and narrow path without distraction. All have sinned. All have come short of the glory of God. All have need of repentance. Thus all of us, to some degree, have taken brief detours from the gospel path, detours that cost us time and opportunity. Christ our Lord leads us back to the path and beckons us to hold more tightly to the rod of iron, to take fewer and fewer excursions from the path, and to rid ourselves of those curiosities with the carnal which can corrupt. He calls us to navigate the narrow passageway to life eternal with caution and care and to seek for that inner stability that fortifies us against the roller-coaster existence so typical of those who are wafted about by the whims of the world.

Disciples of Christ frequently come into the fold from the broad ways of the world. Often they enter the restored Church with much desire but with little ability, with great longing for spiritual encounter but with little capacity and experience. This kingdom is, however, a kingdom of equals, a place for experience, a training ground for saints. Thus a convert's attitude and openness lay the foundation for his spiritual altitude and opportunities. Beginnings are hard but necessary.

And so it is that we need not have a dramatic and earth-shaking conversion in order to become acclimated to the world of the Spirit. In fact, if someone comes into the Church because of such an unusual experience—and some do—then lifetime conversion may well have to come about as much in spite of it as because of it. The quiet whisperings of the Spirit and the settled conviction of the truth are the seedbed for the fruits of faith. Such tender and often tiny tutorials as the Lord grants day in and day out anchor one in the faith. Some, like Paul and Alma and Lamoni, undergo dramatic transformations from death to life. These, however, are the exceptions, and even such people — if they are to remain and continue faithful — come to operate thereafter by the ongoing and generally unseen workings of the Holy Ghost.

Jesus taught in the meridian of time: "If ye *continue* in my word, then are ye my disciples indeed; and ye shall know the truth, and the truth shall make you free" (John 8:31–32; emphasis added.) So often we lay stress upon the latter part of this passage, on the importance of being made free in and through the truth. And that is vital. But let us focus upon the first part of verse 31: "If ye continue in my word." The call to discipleship is a call to continue. To carry on. To persist. To endure. To finish. The Lord needs finishers, those who make the commitment and then walk the road — no matter the difficulty or challenge — to the very end.

The scriptural writers use a word that describes beautifully the stable, consistent, spiritually mature course of the disciple — the word *steadfast*. Peace here and eternal life hereafter are not gained through quantum leaps, marathons, or sudden surges of spirituality. Rather disciples attempt to maintain a regular, constant approach to keeping the commandments and acquiring the attributes of godliness. The Nephite prophets declared that those who looked forward with steadfastness to the coming of Christ would not perish (see 2 Ne. 25:4; 26:8; Alma 5:48; 3 Ne. 1:8) and further explained the need for the people to stand steadfast in their faith and observance of the commandments (Mosiah 4:11; Alma 1:25; Hel. 15:8). "Wherefore," Nephi wrote, "ye must press forward with a steadfastness in Christ, having a perfect brightness of hope, and a love of God and of all men. Wherefore, if ye shall press forward, feasting upon the word of Christ, and endure to the end, behold, thus saith the Father: Ye shall have eternal life" (2 Ne. 31:20).

One virtue evidenced in the life of true disciples, those who are steadfast and consistent, is patience. They are patient with God, "willing to submit to all things which the Lord seeth fit to inflict upon him" (Mosiah 3:19), knowing that "all things work together for good to them that love God" (Rom. 8:28; compare D&C 90:24). Patience is thus closely related to perspective, the ability to see things from a higher elevation. The disciple is patient with Church leaders, trusting implicitly in their prophetic callings and in their ability to discern and declare the word and will of the Lord. True followers of the Christ receive the words of the living oracles "as if from [the Savior's] own mouth, in all patience and faith" (D&C 21:5). The Master calls for intelligent obedience but occasionally for that obedience which is borne of trust and faith. Our attitude might be: "I do not understand the reasons for this action, I do not see clearly what the presiding authorities have in view in doing this, but I will wait and learn more. This I do know, that this is the work of God and that these men are his servants and that they will not be permitted by him to lead the Church astray or to commit a wrong of so serious a character as to endanger its progress or perpetuity."[1] Disciples of Christ learn to be patient with themselves. Though a type of divine discontent pushes disciples to greater heights and causes them to lengthen their stride, yet theirs is "a perfect brightness of hope" (2 Ne. 31:20), a quiet trust in and reliance upon the Lord, a submission to his divine timetable and schedule. "Ye are not able to abide the presence of God now," the Lord explained in 1831, "neither the ministering of angels; wherefore, continue in patience until ye are perfected" (D&C 67:13).

To continue in his word is to seek to live the whole law, to submit to the requirements of the whole gospel. Disciples of Christ do not, for example, decide which of the commandments they will keep. "I believe," Elder Hans B. Ringger said, "that if we want to be true Christians, our lives must be founded upon true principles and our actions must reflect that. But I do not believe that we can pick and choose which principles are the most convenient ones."[2] Nor do true disciples lose their balance in regard to the whole gospel plan, specialize in one phase of Church doctrine or program, develop "gospel hobbies." The Saints of the Most High are commanded to live by every word which proceeds forth from the mouth of God (Matt. 4:4; D&C 84:44). President Joseph F. Smith taught:

"Brethren and sisters, don't have [gospel] hobbies. Hobbies are dangerous in the Church of Christ. They are dangerous because they give undue prominence to certain principles or ideas to the detriment and dwarfing of others just as important, just as binding, just as saving as the favored doctrines or commandments.

"Hobbies give to those who encourage them a false aspect of the gospel of the Redeemer; they distort and place out of harmony its principles and teachings. The point of view is unnatural. Every principle and practice revealed from God is essential to man's salvation, and to place any one of them unduly in front, hiding and dimming all others is unwise and dangerous; it jeopardizes our salvation, for it darkens our minds and beclouds our understandings."[3]

In the same spirit of counsel and warning, Elder Bruce R. McConkie explained: "It is . . . my experience that people who ride gospel hobbies, who try to qualify themselves as experts in some specialized field, who try to make the whole plan of salvation revolve around some field of particular interest to them— it is my experience that such persons are usually spiritually immature and spiritually unstable. This includes those who devote themselves—as though by divine appointment—to setting forth the signs of the times; or to expounding about the Second Coming; or, to a faddist interpretation of the Word of Wisdom; or, to a twisted emphasis on temple work or any other doctrine or practice.

"We would do well," Elder McConkie concluded, "to have a sane, rounded, and balanced approach to the whole gospel and all of its doctrines."[4] "A Christian life demands decision and dedication," Elder Ringger stated. "It is a dedication that is free of fanaticism but full of understanding and love. . . . It is a dedication that embraces all mankind and yet keeps an eye single to the Lord."[5]

In stressing the need for members of the Church to stand by their posts and remain (continue) faithful, Jesus said, "No man, having put his hand to the plough, and looking back, is fit for the kingdom of God" (Luke 9:62). The call to discipleship is a call to stay at our duty stations and complete the task assigned to us. It is to look ahead to our Lord and Savior, following where he leads. It is to give no heed to the enticements and allurements of the perverse, to pay no attention to the unimportant and irrelevant. "O then, my beloved brethren," Jacob wrote, "repent ye, and enter in at the strait gate, and continue in the way which is narrow, until ye shall obtain eternal life" (Jacob 6:11).

NOTES

1. George Q. Cannon, *Juvenile Instructor*, 15 Oct. 1896, p. 618.

2. *Ensign*, May 1990, pp. 25–26.

3. *Gospel Doctrine* (Salt Lake City: Deseret Book Co., 1971), pp. 116–17.

4. In *Doctrines of the Restoration: Sermons and Writings of Bruce R. McConkie*, ed. Mark L. McConkie (Salt Lake City: Bookcraft, 1989), p. 232.

5. *Ensign*, May 1990, p. 26.

Chapter 16

NO MAN BUILDETH A TOWER

Salvation is a gift. Disciples qualify for it, however, through applying the principle of sacrifice. Membership in the Church of Jesus Christ is a serious matter. Followers of the Christ, if they expect eventually to become as he is, must be willing to encounter hardship and pain and suffering, even as their Master did. There is a cost for discipleship.

"And it came to pass, that, as they went in the way, a certain man said unto him, Lord I will follow thee whithersoever thou goest" (Luke 9:57). Truly many people so say. "Lord, I would be with thee," they proclaim. "I would be a true follower." It is as though the Redeemer asks in retort: "Would you really? Do you know what such a life entails? Are you ready to engage the trials, the abuse, the desertion? Are you prepared to pay the price?" The account from Luke continues: "And Jesus said unto him, Foxes have holes, and the birds of the air have nests; but the Son of man hath not where to lay his head" (Luke 9:58). The call to follow is the call to face the stark realities of discipleship—the inconvenience, the impediments, the irony. The mother of James and John once approached the Savior in regard to the future status of her two sons. "She saith unto him, Grant that these my two sons may sit, the one on thy right hand, and the other on the left, in thy kingdom." Our Lord responded soberly: "Ye know not what ye ask." And then he posed the query that must and should echo in the hearts and minds of all who aspire to fellowship with the Son of Man: "Are ye able to drink of the cup that I shall drink of, and to be baptized with the baptism that I am baptized with?" (Matt. 20:20–22).

Jesus asked: "Which of you intending to build a tower, sitteth not down first, and counteth the cost, whether he have money to finish his work? Lest, unhappily, after he has laid the foundation and is not able to finish his work, all who behold, begin to mock him, saying, This man began to build, and was not able to finish. And this he said, signifying there should not any man follow him, unless he was able *to continue*" (JST, Luke 14:29–31; emphasis added). A Protestant theologian has written: "The Christian landscape is strewn with the wreckage of derelict, half-built towers—the ruins of those who began to build and were unable to finish. For thousands of people still ignore Christ's warning and undertake to follow him without first pausing to reflect on the cost of doing so. The result is the great scandal of Christendom today, so-called 'nominal Christianity.' In countries to which Christian civilization has spread, large numbers of people have covered themselves with a decent, but thin, veneer of Christianity. They have allowed themselves to become somewhat involved; enough to be respectable but not enough to be uncomfortable. Their religion is a great, soft cushion. It protects them from the hard unpleasantness of life, while changing its place and shape to suit their convenience. No wonder the cynics speak of hypocrites in the church and dismiss religion as escapism."[1]

Another minister, addressing himself to the problems of a type of "easy-believism" in the world of evangelism, said: "Modern evangelism is preoccupied with decisions, statistics, aisle-walking, gimmicks, prefabricated presentations, pitches, emotional manipulation, and even intimidation. Its message is a cacophony of easy-believism and simplistic appeals. Unbelievers are told that if they invite Jesus into their hearts, accept Him as personal Savior, or believe the facts of the gospel, that's all there is to it. The aftermath is appalling failure, as seen in the lives of multitudes who have professed faith in Christ with no consequent impact on their behavior."[2]

The cost of discipleship must be understood by converts. "Occasionally someone is attracted to the Church," Elder Boyd K. Packer observed, "because of our welfare program. They see material security. Our answer to them is: 'Yes, join the Church for that reason. We can use all of the help we can get. You will be called upon continually to bless and assist others.' Interesting how enthusiasm for baptism often fades away."[3] The cost must also be understood by lifetime members, for the earnest investigator and the convert are not the only ones who will be called upon to erect towers of testimony. Nor are they the only ones required to enter the battleground of faith. "What king, going to make war against another king, sitteth not down first, and consulteth whether he be able with ten thousand, to meet him who cometh against him with twenty thousand. Or else, while the other is yet a great way off, he sendeth an embassage, and desireth conditions of peace." And then the Master's powerful precept: "So likewise, whosoever of you forsaketh not all that he hath he cannot be my disciple" (JST, Luke 14:32–34).

The word of truth is as sharp and powerful as a two-edged sword. It is no respecter of persons, nor does its cutting power stop short of tender and dear relations. "Think not that I am come to send peace on earth," the Prince of Peace declared; "I came not to send peace, but a sword. For I am come to set a man at variance against his father, and the daughter against her mother, and the daughter in law against her mother in law. And a man's foes shall be they of his own household. He that loveth father or mother more than me is not worthy of me: and he that loveth son or daughter more than me is not worthy of me" (Matt. 10: 34–37). There is a pathetic irony in the Savior's words. Surely no one wants families to be forever, joined and united, more than Jesus. No one wants father and mother, brother and sister, parents and children—families—to be close and at peace more than the Christ. And yet the Lord here highlights a less than pleasant point—that gospel living costs something, even occasionally the loss of family and friends. It may well result in division and variance.

Not all people in our day will receive the testimony of Jesus and the message of the Restoration nor will family members always support and sustain the loved one who chooses to follow his or her heart. Baptism into the Church may well be followed by resistance, by indifference, or even by persecution. Such is a painful and poignant reality. It is a heavy cost. With startling emphasis the Savior thus declared: "If any man come to me, and hate not his father, and mother, and wife, and children, and brethren, and sisters, or husband, yea and his own life also; or *in other words, is afraid to lay down his life for my sake*; cannot be my disciple" (JST, Luke 14:26; emphasis added). President Gordon B. Hinckley related a touching story that illustrates dramatically the cost of discipleship.

"Mine has been the opportunity to meet many wonderful men and women in various parts of the world. A few of them have left an indelible impression upon me. One such was a naval officer from Asia, a brilliant young man who had been brought to the United States for advanced training. Some of his associates in the United States Navy, whose behavior had attracted him, shared with him at his request their religious beliefs. He was not a Christian, but he was interested. They told him of the Savior of the world, of Jesus born in Bethlehem, who gave his life for all mankind. They told him of the appearance of God, the Eternal Father, and the resurrected Lord to the boy Joseph Smith. They spoke of modern prophets. They taught him the gospel of the Master. The Spirit touched his heart, and he was baptized.

"He was introduced to me just before he was to return to his native land. We spoke of these things, and then I said, 'Your people are not Christians. You come from a land where Christians have had a difficult time. What will happen when you return home a Christian and, more particularly, a Mormon Christian?'

"His face clouded, and he replied, 'My family will be disappointed. I suppose they will cast me out. They will regard me as dead. As for my future and my career, I assume that all opportunity will be foreclosed against me.'

"I asked, 'Are you willing to pay so great a price for the gospel?'

"His dark eyes, moistened by tears, shone from his handsome brown face as he answered, 'It's true, isn't it?'

"Ashamed at having asked the question, I responded, 'Yes, it's true.'

"To which he replied, 'Then what else matters?' "[4]

Joining and being a part of the true Church may not require martyrdom. It may not be followed by persecution or even rejection. But it might. Disciples must be *willing* to submit to whatever following the Master and the counsel of living oracles might entail. Regularly and consistently disciples will be asked to attend meetings and training sessions (and to support with time and patience loved ones who must do the same), to go on campouts, to work in canneries and on farms, and to contribute financially in tithes and offerings. We are called upon to visit and minister to ward or branch members, to clothe the naked and feed the hungry—in general, to lift and liberate and lighten the burdens of others, to be willing to be inconvenienced.

Eternal life, the glory of the celestial kingdom, life with God—these things cannot be had through living a life of ease. The cost of discipleship is not cheap, nor is the saving grace of Him who bought us with his blood to be reckoned as a little thing. "Cheap grace is grace without discipleship, grace without the cross, grace without Jesus Christ, living and incarnate. Costly grace is the treasure hidden in the field; for the sake of it a man will gladly go and sell all that he has. . . . It is costly because it costs a man his life, and it is grace because it gives a man the only true life. . . . Above all, it is costly because it cost God the life of his Son . . . and what has cost God much cannot be cheap for us."[5] And yet the God of the ancients holds out to us the prize: "Verily I say unto you, There is no man that hath left house, or parents, or brethren, or wife, or children, for the kingdom of God's sake, who shall not receive manifold more in

this present time, and in the world to come life everlasting"
(Luke 18:29–30).

NOTES

1. John R. W. Stott, *Basic Christianity* (London: Inter-Varsity Press, 1958), p. 108.

2. John F. MacArthur, Jr., *The Gospel According to Jesus* (Grand Rapids, Mich.: Zondervan, 1988), p. 79.

3. In Conference Report, Apr. 1978, p. 136.

4. In Conference Report, Apr. 1973, p. 72.

5. Dietrich Bonhoeffer, *The Cost of Discipleship*, rev. ed. (New York: Macmillan, 1963), pp. 47–48.

Chapter 17

YE SHALL BE EVEN AS I AM

Fellowship with the Saints and a growing acquaintance with the Spirit should do more than build our understanding of theology. Belonging to the true Church and affiliating with those who have come out of the world should affect our hearts as much as or more than our minds. Religion is a thing of the heart, and the gospel of Jesus Christ has been restored to make of us new creatures, new creatures in Christ, men and women whose lives mirror the matchless life of the one perfect Being. What we know and believe should and must affect what we feel and what we do.

"The highest of all ideals," President David O. McKay taught, "are the teachings and particularly the life of Jesus of Nazareth, and that man is most truly great who is most Christlike.

"What you sincerely in your heart think of Christ will determine what you are, will largely determine what your acts will be. No person can study this divine personality, can accept his teachings without becoming conscious of an uplifting and refining influence within himself. . . . Members of the Church of Jesus Christ are under obligation to make the sinless Son of Man their ideal—the one perfect Being who ever walked the earth."[1] Peter therefore explained that our Savior "suffered for us, leaving us an example, that [we] should follow his steps" (1 Pet. 2:21).

Those who forsake the world, who enter the waters of baptism to evidence their desires to eschew the world, and who take upon them the name of Jesus Christ — these should live and speak and act differently from those who have not yet come unto Christ. Latter-day Saints must be different. If the major distinguishing characteristics of the Mormons are that they refrain from smoking and drinking and that they believe in strong families — nothing more — then we have little to offer the religious world. We have no monopoly on family programs, and we are certainly not the only people in the world who believe that we should take proper care of the physical body. What we believe should and must affect what we do. The gospel, the power of God unto salvation (Rom. 1:16), either has the power to change us or it does not. Thus our true nature — our character, our personality, even our disposition — shows through, and is the best evidence of how well we have incorporated the principles and attributes of divinity into our walk and talk. We cannot rightly divide our theology from our religion, our beliefs from our behaviors. No one of us is perfect, to be sure. And yet, there just simply ought to be something different about us as a result of our having the gospel in our lives, something different about the way we treat one another.

Jesus our Lord placed people first. People before programs, people before rules and regulations. For example, "the sabbath was made for man," he said, "and not man for the sabbath" (Mark 2:27). There must be order and cleanliness in the kingdom of God, and members of the Church are expected to abide by the laws and statutes of a divinely established institution. The Church was restored for the benefit and blessing and edification of man. The Church is the auxiliary given to bless and sustain individuals and families. Jesus our Lord also placed people before his own convenience. Jesus "went into the borders of Tyre and Sidon, and entered into a house, and would that no man should come unto him." He was tired. He was weary. He needed, as do we all occasionally, a moment to himself. "But he could not deny them; for he had compassion upon all men" (JST, Mark 7:22–23). The work and glory of God are to bring to pass the immortality and eternal life of man (Moses 1:39). That is, God's

91

work is people. People are ends in themselves, never means, no matter how noble the desired end.

How we act in supermarket lines, in our homes and with family members, on the crowded highway, or at the ballpark— surely those actions bespeak volumes about who and what we are. Disciples, followers of the Christ, have covenanted to allow their religion to be seen and felt on all days and at all times. Disciples come to be sensitive, caring, solicitous. James Allen, in his book *As a Man Thinketh*, has suggested that "circumstance does not make the man; it reveals him to himself."[2] In that regard, C. S. Lewis has offered the following painful but pertinent insights into who and what we are:

"When I come to my evening prayers and try to reckon up the sins of the day, nine times out of ten the most obvious one is some sin against charity; I have sulked or snapped or sneered or snubbed or stormed. And the excuse that immediately springs to my mind is that the provocation was so sudden and unexpected: I was caught off my guard, I had not time to collect myself. Now that may be an extenuating circumstance as regards those particular acts: they would obviously be worse if they had been deliberate and premeditated. On the other hand, surely what a man does when he is taken off his guard is the best evidence for what sort of man he is? Surely what pops out before the man has time to put on a disguise is the truth? If there are rats in a cellar you are most likely to see them if you go in very suddenly. But the suddenness does not create the rats: it only prevents them from hiding. In the same way the suddenness of the provocation does not make me an ill-tempered man: it only shows me what an ill-tempered man I am."[3] Christ came to earth and restored his gospel in our day so that we might become as he is, not alone in belief but also in attitude and action. President Ezra Taft Benson related a story that focuses on that matter:

"There was a little crippled boy who ran a small newsstand in a crowded railroad station. He must have been about twelve years old. Every day he would sell papers, candy, gum, and magazines to the thousands of commuters passing through the terminal.

"One night two men were rushing through the crowded station to catch a train. One was fifteen or twenty yards in front of the other. It was Christmas eve. Their train was scheduled to depart in a matter of minutes.

"The first man turned a corner and in his haste to get home to a Christmas cocktail party plowed right into the little crippled boy. He knocked him off his stool, and candy, newspapers, and gum were scattered everywhere. Without so much as stopping, he cursed the little fellow for being there and rushed on to catch the train that would take him to celebrate Christmas in the way he had chosen for himself.

"It was only a matter of seconds before the second commuter arrived on the scene. He stopped, knelt, and gently picked up the boy. After making sure the child was unhurt, the man gathered up the scattered newspapers, sweets, and magazines. Then he took his wallet and gave the boy a five-dollar bill. 'Son,' he said, 'I think this will take care of what was lost or soiled. Merry Christmas!'

"Without waiting for a reply, the commuter now picked up his briefcase and started to hurry away. As he did, the little crippled boy cupped his hands together and called out, 'Mister, Mister!'

"The man stopped as the boy asked, 'Are you Jesus Christ?'

"By the look on his face, it was obvious the commuter was embarrassed by the question. But he smiled and said, 'No, son, I am not Jesus Christ. But I am trying hard to do what He would do if He were here.' "[4]

A number of years ago Charles M. Sheldon wrote a remarkable book entitled *In His Steps* about a man who decided to take seriously the Savior's injunction to live our religion. A Christian minister, impressed with the thought that the Master meant what he said when he invited us to be even as He is, challenged his congregation to make a significant pledge—a pledge that for one year they would not do anything without first asking the question, "What would Jesus do?" The story is a marvelous study in human nature as well as a testimony of the power of Christ to change human souls. It illustrates the costs and challenges and rewards of Christian discipleship. We might ask ourselves: How does following the example of my Savior affect the way I perform my service in the Church? My service in the community? How does my commitment to emulate the Lord bear upon the way I interact with those I work with in the Church? Those outside the Church? If, indeed, I were arrested on the charge of being a Christian, would there be, as someone has asked, enough evidence to convict me?

What, then, is my pattern for Christian living? How do I know what to do in every case? We are blessed to have the scriptures, particularly the four Gospels, which are testimonies of our Lord's mortal ministry. We see in experience after experience how he acted and reacted to circumstances in his life. The other books of scripture, especially the Book of Mormon, detail and delineate principles and practices, guidelines for living a Christlike life. But the Gospels contain only about a month, about thirty days, of our Savior's thirty-three years. And the other volumes of holy writ cannot provide a circumscribed course in Christianity, cannot possibly give the answer to every question we may face. No, the scriptures teach us principles, precepts which may direct our thinking and channel our resolve in a myriad of situations. Further, as members of the Church we are entitled to the gift of the Holy Ghost, that blessed moral monitor that, often working through our consciences, has been given to teach us how to proceed. The Holy Ghost is, as Joseph Smith explained, the oldest book of living scripture available to us.[5] Nephi instructed, "Feast upon the words of Christ; for behold, the words of Christ will tell you all things what ye should do." Further, "If ye will enter in by the way," Nephi implored, "and receive the Holy Ghost, it will show unto you all things what ye should do" (2 Ne. 32:3, 5).

Finally, it is important to acknowledge that whatever changes need to be made in our character—whether in our speech, our ability to control our temper, our "sins against charity" — can be made in a lasting way only through the intervention of divine powers. Behavior modification programs are not enough. Dogged determination is not enough. Time management and goal-setting programs are not enough. Gritting our teeth and holding on in white-knuckled fashion may not be the answer. As helpful as certain human plans and procedures may be — and as important as it is that I do all in my power to bring about meaningful change in my nature — it is the Redeemer that recreates men and women. As President Ezra Taft Benson pointed out, "The Lord works from the inside out. The world works from the outside in. The world would take people out of the slums. Christ takes the slums out of people, and then they take themselves out of the slums. The world would mold men by changing their environment. Christ changes men, who then change their environment. The world would shape human behavior, but Christ can change human nature."[6]

"If . . . what we are matters even more than what we do," C. S. Lewis observed, "if, indeed, what we do matters chiefly as evidence of what we are — then it follows that the change which I most need to undergo is a change which my own direct, voluntary efforts cannot bring about. . . . I cannot, by direct moral effort, give myself new motives. After the first few steps in the Christian life we realize that everything which really needs to be done in our souls can be done only by God."[7] That is surely what the Lord meant when he spoke to Moroni: "If men come unto me I will show unto them their weakness. I give unto men weakness that they may be humble; and my grace is sufficient for all men that humble themselves before me; for if they humble themselves before me, and have faith in me, then will I make weak things become strong unto them" (Ether 12:27).

It just may be that the depth of our discipleship is not to be gauged by how quickly we could prepare to leave for Missouri, or how bravely we would face the barrel of a mobster's rifle. Perhaps one of the real tests of our discipleship is the degree to which we have sought for and allowed the powers of Deity to change our hearts, renovate our souls, and point us toward people. "Ye shall be even as I am," the risen Messiah said to the Nephites, "and I am even as the Father; and the Father and I are one" (3 Ne. 28:10). As we become one with him, we come to love and forgive and extend ourselves to those who need us. Disciples are called upon to love others and to minister in their behalf. In the process they come to love others more than themselves. That is the essence of Christianity.

NOTES

1. *Gospel Ideals* (Salt Lake City: Improvement Era, 1953), pp. 34–35.

2. Cited in Spencer W. Kimball, *The Miracle of Forgiveness* (Salt Lake City: Bookcraft, 1969), p. 105.

3. *Mere Christianity* (New York: Macmillan, 1952), pp. 164–65.

4. Cited in *Come unto Christ* (Salt Lake City: Deseret Book Co., 1983), pp. 42–43.

5. *Teachings of the Prophet Joseph Smith*, sel. Joseph Fielding Smith (Salt Lake City: Deseret Book Co., 1976), p. 349.

6. In Conference Report, Oct. 1985, p. 5.

7. *Mere Christianity*, p. 165.

Chapter 18

SEEK YE FIRST
THE KINGDOM OF GOD

One challenge we face on earth is to remember why we do what we do. It is not easy in a world with distractions, many of which seem to be good and noble and upright, to remain focused on fundamentals and riveted on matters of everlasting consequence. The duty of disciples is to discern and, where necessary, to discard. Knowing that we cannot do everything, the follower of the Nazarene chooses to do that which is of greatest worth. In a day when discordant voices clamor for attention, we attend ever so carefully to that voice, still and small, which offers unerring direction.

In the Sermon on the Mount, the Savior said: "The light of the body is the eye; if therefore thine eye be single to the glory of God, thy whole body shall be full of light. But if thine eye be evil, thy whole body shall be full of darkness. If therefore the light which is in thee be darkness, how great shall that darkness be" (JST, Matt. 6:22–23). The word *eye* is frequently used in scripture to represent the heart, the disposition, the mind. When our mind is single to the glory of God, our hearts and feelings are focused upon the things that God considers important. Moses was told of the glory of God: "This is my work and my glory," Jehovah declared, "to bring to pass the immortality and eternal life of man" (Moses 1:39). To have an eye single to the glory of God is thus to be working toward that same grand goal—the immortality and eternal life of ourselves, our families, and all of the other sons and daughters of God. It is to have placed the

97

ego on the altar of life and presented an offering to the Almighty, even that of a broken heart and a contrite spirit (3 Ne. 9:20; D&C 59:8). To have an eye single to the glory of God is to have sacrificed self in behalf of the greater good.

When we have an eye single to the glory of God we are more concerned with conversions than baptisms, honesty and inspiration than with good impressions, edifying meetings than with statistics, covenant and commitment than with position and office. Spiritual power comes to those who focus on fundamentals. Elder Dean L. Larsen observed that "the enduring strength of the kingdom is not to be found in the number of its members, the rate of its growth, or the beauty of its buildings. In God's kingdom, power is not equated with body count nor with outward routine compliance with prescribed performances. It is found in those quiet uncharted acts of love, obedience, and Christian service which may never come to the attention of official leadership, but which emulate the ministry of the Lord himself."[1] The sanctifying powers of the Spirit flow into the lives of individuals and congregations who yield their hearts to God (Hel. 3:35). "And if your eye be single to my glory, your whole bodies shall be filled with light, and there shall be no darkness in you; and that body which is filled with light comprehendeth all things. Therefore, sanctify yourselves that your minds [note the equation of eye with mind] become single to God, and the days will come that you shall see him" (D&C 88:67–68).

Disciples seek for discernment, not alone to tell good from evil but also to sort out the less important from the more important, the fascinating from the vital. Elder Bruce R. McConkie addressed this challenge:

"I am fully aware of the divine decree to be actively engaged in a good cause; of the fact that every true principle which works for the freedom and blessing of mankind has the Lord's approval; of the need to sustain and support those who espouse proper causes and advocate true principles—all of which things we also should do in the best and most beneficial way we can. The issue, I think, is not what we should do but how we should do it; and

I maintain that the most beneficial and productive thing which Latter-day Saints can do to strengthen every good and proper cause is to live and teach the principles of the everlasting gospel.

"There may be those who have special gifts and needs to serve in other fields, but as far as I am concerned with the knowledge and testimony that I have, there is nothing I can do for the time and season of this mortal probation, that is more important than to use all my strength, energy and ability in spreading and perfecting the cause of truth and righteousness, both in the Church and among our Father's other children."[2]

The disciple of Christ must be disciplined not only in regard to the sordid but also in regard to the subsidiary. Some things matter more than others, and there simply isn't enough time in this life to do everything, especially to labor in secondary causes. The scriptures and the modern prophets have provided the guidelines for us. The Church will teach us the principles, and the Holy Ghost will reveal to us the specific practices.

The renewed emphasis by the Brethren upon the mission of the Church, the invitation to come unto Christ, the need to simplify and reduce—these things attest to the seeric vision of those called to direct the destiny of this Church. The greater emphasis upon covenants and ordinances also points up our duty to center our lives in Christ, receive and be true to those saving principles and rites that weld us to Christ and to our families, and invite all others to go and do likewise. Those Saints whose teachings and lives reflect the principle of covenant will be as a lighthouse in the midst of a stormy sea. Elder Boyd K. Packer taught this lesson to the Church in the following way:

"Several years ago I installed a stake president in England. In another calling, he is here in the audience today. He had an unusual sense of direction. He was like a mariner with a sextant who took his bearings from the stars. I met with him each time he came to conference and was impressed that he kept himself and his stake on course.

"Fortunately for me, when it was time for his release, I was assigned to reorganize the stake. It was then that I discovered what that sextant was and how he adjusted it to check his position and get a bearing for himself and for his members.

"He accepted his release, and said: 'I was happy to accept the call to serve as stake president, and I am equally happy to accept my release. I did not serve just because I was under *call*. I served because I am under *covenant*. And I can keep my covenants quite as well as a home teacher as I can serving as stake president.'

"This president understood the word *covenant*.

"While he was neither a scriptorian nor a gospel scholar, he somehow had learned that exaltation is achieved by keeping covenants, not by holding high position."[3]

We can probably have our share of this world's goods if we want them. Some of the pressing questions we must face, however, are the following: Why do I want them? What function will they serve? Will they prove a blessing or a condemnation? The prophetic invitation is: "Think of your brethren like unto yourselves, and be familiar with all and free with your substance, that they may be rich like unto you. But *before ye seek for riches, seek ye for the kingdom of God*. And after ye have obtained a hope in Christ ye shall obtain riches, if ye seek them; and ye will seek them for the intent to do good—to clothe the naked, and to feed the hungry, and to liberate the captive, and administer relief to the sick and the afflicted" (Jacob 2:17–19; emphasis added).

If we seek first for the kingdom of God—commit ourselves to the Church and strive to be loyal to its constituted authorities, to the care of the needy, to the support of missionaries, and so forth—then our hearts are more prone to be pure, and we are more likely to deal properly and prudently with our monetary gain. In Jacob's words, disciples will seek to be prospered in order to assist others. The Old Testament records a chilling story of a prophet named Balaam who enjoyed for a season the favor and confidence of God but who, because he "loved the wages of unrighteousness," lost his birthright and fell from his high standing (see Num. 22–25, 31). Balaam knew exactly what the Lord wanted him to do, but greed and avarice turned his heart toward the god of this world. Elder Bruce R. McConkie has written of this tragic incident:

"Perhaps the Lord would let him compromise his standards and have some worldly prosperity and power as well as a testimony of the gospel. Of course he knew the gospel was true, as it were, but why should he be denied the things his political file leader could confer?

"I wonder how often some of us get our direction from the Church and then, Balaam-like, plead for some worldly rewards and finally receive an answer which says, in effect, If you are determined to be a millionaire or to gain this or that worldly honor, go ahead, with the understanding that you will continue to serve the Lord. Then we wonder why things don't work out for us as well as they would have done if we had put first in our lives the things of God's kingdom.

"What are the rewards of unrighteousness? Do they not include seeking for worldly things when these run counter to the interests of the Church?

"And don't we all know people who, though they were once firm and steadfast in testimony, are now opposing the Lord's purposes and interests on earth because money and power have twisted their judgment of what should or should not be?

"Balaam, the prophet, inspired and mighty as he once was, lost his soul in the end because he set his heart on the things of this world rather than the riches of eternity."[4]

One of the remarkable ironies of gospel living is that we become totally free only as we submit to the will of the Lord. The plain fact is that God knows what is best for us; he can make so much more out of us than we can through our own unaided efforts. Loving God with all our hearts—keeping the first and great commandment—entails seeking and acknowledging his hand and striving to live in harmony with the plan he has established for our eternal happiness. As we come to have an eye single to the glory of God, our will begins to become God's will; our desires become God's; our joys and sorrows, God's. Truly, as President Ezra Taft Benson explained, *"The great test of life is* obedience to God. . . . *The great task of life* is to learn the will of the Lord and then do it. *The great commandment of life* is to love the Lord." In reality, "When we put God first, all other things fall into their proper place or drop out of our lives. Our love of the Lord will govern the claims for our affection, the demands on our time, the interests we pursue, and the order of our priorities. We should put God ahead of *everyone else* in our lives."[5]

We are from another time, another place, another world. We do not have permanent residence here, at least not in this telestial tenement. When the Savior counseled his disciples to "take no thought for the morrow," what they should eat or drink or wear, he was warning against becoming too acclimated to a fallen sphere, warning against earthly anxiety and attachment to this world's worries and enticements. He who never owned a home does not ask of those who follow him to live as paupers, to exist on a subsistence level only. He does not delight in the financial struggles of his people, nor does he take pleasure in the material challenges his disciples inevitably face in a materialistic world. But he does ask that his disciples refuse to give prominence to the things of this world. He pleads with his servants to see to it that their hearts are set on nobler pursuits. No wiser and more appropriate charge, therefore, could be given the disciple than the one that states: "Seek not the things of this world, but seek ye first to build up the kingdom of God, and to establish his righteousness, and all these things" — the necessities and comforts of life — "shall be added unto you" (JST, Matt. 6:38).

NOTES

1. In Conference Report, Oct. 1981, p. 38.
2. In Conference Report, Oct. 1973, p. 55.
3. In Conference Report, Apr. 1987, pp. 26–27; emphasis in original.
4. *New Era*, Apr. 1972, p. 7.
5. In Conference Report, Apr. 1988, p. 3; emphasis in original.

THE FRUITS OF DISCIPLESHIP

Chapter 19

MY PEOPLE WILL I PRESERVE

Disciples of the last days shall live to see a growing chasm between good and evil. The polarization between those who confess Christ before men—and thus shall be acknowledged and recommended by their Redeemer hereafter—and those who deny and defy the truth—and thus become those whom the Master shall deny and condemn hereafter (see Matt. 10:32–33)—will intensify as we approach the millennial day. The follower of the Lord is called upon to exercise discernment, to read by the lamp of the Spirit, and to know and recognize the signs of the times.

To read the signs of the times is to perceive the unfolding of God's divine drama in the final days of earth's temporal continuance; it is to have a total perspective of the plan of life and salvation and a special appreciation for the scenes incident to its consummation. It is to understand that this is the day long awaited by the prophets of old and by the messengers of heaven, when God would pour out knowledge and power from on high "by the unspeakable gift of the Holy Ghost," knowledge "that has not been revealed since the world was until now" (D&C 121:26).

On the other hand, to read the signs of the times in our day is to read the signs of wear and tear in the countenances of those who have chosen to love and give devoted service to questionable or diabolical causes. Error and wickedness take their terrible tolls upon the hearts of those who choose divergent paths; the wheels of waywardness grind away slowly but inexorably to produce a type of demented character that will never know peace of mind. To read the signs of the times is, in part, to acknowledge the profundity of Alma's words that "wickedness never was happiness" (Alma 41:10).

To read the signs of the times in this era of time is to make a decision in favor of Zion and the Church of the Lamb or in favor of Babylon and the church of the devil (1 Ne. 14:10). Each city, Zion and Babylon, makes definite requirements of its citizens, and as the end approaches, each community will insist upon the total devotion and consecration of its municipals. To read the signs of the times is to recognize that in the future fewer and fewer Latter-day Saints will be "lukewarm"; that the myopic and the misguided of the religious world will grow in cynicism and confusion; that the ungodly will, as time goes by, sink ever deeper into a despair known only to those who revel in iniquity; and that wickedness will widen and malevolence multiply until the citizens of Babylon seal themselves to him who is the father of all lies (see 2 Ne. 9:46; Alma 34:34–35; Hel. 13:32).

To read the signs of the times is to become aware also that "Zion must arise and put on her beautiful garments" (D&C 82:14); that the Church of the Lamb shall continue to require the tithes and offerings of its members until that day when a fully consecrated life is required; and that through giving all to the Lord through his Church, the Saints of the Most High shall establish a heaven on earth and eventually receive the glorious assurance of exaltation in the highest heaven.

The future of The Church of Jesus Christ of Latter-day Saints is glorious. Many living now will see the day when those of all walks of life and from all parts of the earth, by the millions, will enter the waters of baptism and covenant to become true followers of the Christ. Temples shall dot the earth, as the prophets have foretold, and the blessings of Abraham, Isaac, and Jacob—those blessings which qualify men and women to become kings and queens, priests and priestesses, shall be available to all nations, kindreds, tongues, and peoples (Rev. 5:9–10). And yet, as the work of the Lord goes forward in accelerated fashion, as the tent of Zion begins to have its stakes driven into the soil in every corner of the globe, so also shall the work of Beelzebub go forward. Nephi saw in vision that the whore of all the earth sat upon many waters, meaning she was found in every land (Rev. 17:15) and had dominion over all the earth (1 Ne. 14:11).

"The vision of the future," Elder Bruce R. McConkie warned, "is not all sweetness and light and peace. All [the good] that is yet to be shall go forward in the midst of greater evils and perils and desolations than have been known on earth at any time."[1] After having beheld in vision the destruction of gross wickedness in the days of his descendant Noah, Enoch cried out to God: "When shall the earth rest?" When shall the Son of Man appear to bring to an end the violence and vile affections on the face of the earth? "And the Lord said unto Enoch: As I live, even so will I come in the last days, in the days of wickedness and vengeance. . . . And the day shall come that the earth shall rest, but before that day the heavens shall be darkened, and a veil of darkness shall cover the earth; and the heavens shall shake, and also the earth; and great tribulations shall be among the children of men, but *my people will I preserve*" (Moses 7:58–61; emphasis added). The veil of darkness, the apostasy and wickedness of the final days, is before us. And in the midst of it all, disciples are called upon to stand fast in the faith. The Savior taught his Galilean Twelve: "There shall be men standing in that genera-tion" – the time wherein the signs pertaining to the second com-ing of Christ are fulfilled – "that shall not pass until they shall see an overflowing scourge; for a desolating sickness shall cover the land." And then Jesus offered this glimmer of hope: "But my disciples shall stand in holy places, and shall not be moved; but among the wicked, men shall lift up their voices and curse God and die" (D&C 45:31–32; emphasis added).

Disciples, to be preserved from the calamities yet to come, must stand in holy places. And what are holy places? An obvious illustration of holy places is temples. The Saints remain Saints only to the degree that they receive and remain worthy of the covenants, ordinances, and instruction within the temples. The temple is the central focus of Zion. In the temple, we are schooled in the mysteries of godliness and made acquainted with a higher form of learning—learning by faith and obedience. The temple is a place of covenant, a place of renewal and recommitment, and a place of instruction, heavenly instruction. "It has become my conviction," said Elder F. Enzio Busche, "that the temple is the only 'university' for men to prepare spiritually for their graduation to eternal life. The temple is the place where the Lord wants us to make a sincere evaluation of our mortal lives. . . . We are still alive, and our probationary state is not yet over. Temples have been erected as houses of the Lord. They are standing ready to serve as instruments to our own gradual awakening to the full dimensions of truth on our inevitable road to eternity."[2] As the intersection between the heavens and the earth, the holy temple, with its ordinances and instruction, helps to serve as a cold but gentle slap in the face for mortal men and women, an ever-present reminder of what matters most.

The church is a holy place. Those who attend regularly, take part, and find joy in its service agencies, gain the comfort and confidence to withstand opposition and discern the inroads of a morally bankrupt society. There are those, sadly, who hold membership in the Church but who feel some embarrassment about it. They feel the Church should be more progressive, more pluralistic and open to religious diversity, less "dogmatic" and more ecumenical. They are deceived and know not what they ask. To tear the Church up from its bedrock of revelation or to break its tie to absolute truths is to be a part of the shared impotence, the rational relativity of a world that has no sure foundation. It is to trade our birthright for the pan in which was once a mess of pottage. No, the restored Church has been established as an ensign, a banner around which battle-weary Saints may gather; it is a defense, a refuge "from the storm, and from wrath when it shall be poured out without mixture upon the whole earth" (D&C 115:6). In speaking of the importance of holding fast to time-honored and revealed practices within the

Church, Elder Boyd K. Packer said: "I would remind [you] that it is not the privilege of those called as leaders to slide the Church about as though it were on casters, hoping to put it into the path that men or youth will be safe within it."[3] In order to keep themselves unspotted from the sins of the world, then, disciples are to attend church, "go to the house of prayer and offer up [their] sacraments upon [the Lord's] holy day" (D&C 59:9). In speaking of the New Jerusalem, the center place of Zion, a modern revelation attested: "And the glory of the Lord shall be there, and the terror of the Lord also shall be there, insomuch that the wicked will not come unto it, and it shall be called Zion. And it shall come to pass among the wicked, that every man that will not take his sword against his neighbor must needs flee unto Zion for safety" (D&C 45:67-68). "The time is nigh," President Brigham Young warned in regard to this scriptural passage, "when every man that will not take up his sword against his neighbor must needs flee to Zion. Where is Zion? Where the organization of the Church of God is."[4]

The home is a holy place. In fact, the Lord intends that the home become the holiest of all. Our service and involvement in the temple and the church should but prepare us for our labors in the home. President Harold B. Lee reminded us often that the most important work we would ever do in the Church would be within the walls of our own homes.[5] The family is the most important unit in time and in eternity, and the home is the place, the setting, where family members are taught, nurtured, built up, prepared, and immunized against a spiritually hostile world. True followers of Christ sense the significance of the home and thus devote time and talents and energies to the creation of a clean, peaceful, and spiritually rewarding environment therein.

Finally, disciples stand in holy places whenever they are striving to live a life of holiness—to enjoy the revelatory and cleansing powers of the Holy Ghost and to be loyal and true to those called to direct the destiny of the Church and kingdom. President Harold B. Lee spoke of his visit to a group of Saints during the frightening times of a world war:

"I heard a group of anxious people asking, 'Is now the day for us to come up to Zion, where we can come to the mountain of the Lord, where we can be protected from our enemies?' I pondered that question, I prayed about it. What should we say to those people who were in their anxiety? I have studied it a bit, I have learned something of what the Spirit has taught, and I know now that the place of safety in this world is not in any given place; it doesn't make so much difference *where* we live; but the all-important thing is *how* we live, and I have found that the security can come to Israel only when they keep the commandments, when they live so they can enjoy the companionship, the direction, the comfort, and the guidance of the Holy Spirit of the Lord, when they are willing to listen to these men whom God has set here to preside as His mouthpieces, and when we obey the counsels of the Church."[6]

The heaven-sent promise that the Lord would preserve his people in the last days, in the midst of wickedness and vengeance, is not necessarily a promise that all will be spared death. Rather, the assurance is that the disciple need not fear death, if such is required, as long as he or she is in the line of duty. "We do not say," Elder McConkie pointed out, "that all of the Saints will be spared and saved from the coming day of desolation. But we do say there is no promise of safety and no promise of security except for those who love the Lord and who are seeking to do all that he commands."[7] Thus saith the Lord: "Behold, it is my will, that all they who call on my name, and worship me according to mine everlasting gospel, should gather together, and stand in holy places; and prepare for the revelation which is to come, when the veil of the covering of my temple, in my tabernacle, which hideth the earth, shall be taken off, and all flesh shall see me together" (D&C 101:22–23).

NOTES

1. In Conference Report, Apr. 1980, p. 99.
2. In Conference Report, Apr. 1989, pp. 89, 91.

3. In Conference Report, Oct. 1973, p. 22.

4. *Journal of Discourses*, 26 vols. (Liverpool: F. D. Richards, 1851–86), 8:205; see also *Teachings of the Prophet Joseph Smith*, sel. Joseph Fielding Smith (Salt Lake City: Deseret Book Co., 1976), pp. 160–61.

5. See *Ye Are the Light of the World* (Salt Lake City: Deseret Book Co., 1974), pp. 33, 80; *Decisions for Successful Living* (Salt Lake City: Deseret Book Co., 1973), p. 248.

6. In Conference Report, Apr. 1943, p. 129; emphasis added.

7. In Conference Report, Apr. 1979, p. 133.

Chapter 20

THE TRUTH SHALL
MAKE YOU FREE

To be unaware or uninterested in truth—of "the knowledge of things as they are, and as they were, and as they are to come" (D&C 93:24)—is to lead a sheltered and shallow existence. It is to be in bondage, to be stifled. To be oblivious to that which the Spirit teaches, namely the truth—"things as they really are, and . . . things as they really will be" (Jacob 4:13)—is to be damned. Christ came to deliver us from ourselves and from Satan, to liberate us from the chains of darkness and doubt and deceit. "Then said Jesus to those Jews which believed on him, If ye continue in my word, then are ye my disciples indeed; and ye shall know the truth, and the truth shall make you free" (John 8:31–32).

The revelations of the Restoration certify that certain truths are known only by faithfulness. To say that another way, there are some matters that may only be comprehended, and even apprehended, by righteousness, some things a wicked or careless person will never know. My friend and colleague, Joseph F. McConkie, observed: "Purity, not intellect, is the prime requisite for the knowledge of God. Knowledge that can be obtained independent of purity and righteousness is without the power of salvation. Only that knowledge that comes from God through the medium of the Holy Spirit has the power to sanctify the soul and prepare one to stand in the divine presence. Such is the

112

'Spirit of truth,' a spirit which the 'world cannot receive' (John 14:17)."[1] The scriptures state that "he that keepeth [the Lord's] commandments receiveth truth and light, until he is glorified in truth and knoweth all things" (D&C 93:28). Joseph Smith likewise explained that "whatever principle of intelligence we attain unto in this life, it will rise with us in the resurrection. And if a person gains more knowledge and intelligence in this life *through his diligence and obedience* than another, he will have so much the advantage in the world to come" (D&C 130:18–19; emphasis added).

Surely we are put here on earth to learn as much as we can in the sciences, in the arts, in languages, in history and foreign culture, and so on. And, to the degree that we can master some of these fields, we are better able to present the gospel and its truths in a manner that would be acceptable to more and more people (see D&C 88:78–80). But there is a hierarchy of truth. Some truths matter more than others. It is valuable to know of gravity or of the laws of motion. It is vital to know of the reality of a Redeemer. It is helpful to know the laws of thermodynamics; it is essential to know how to repent and call upon God, in the name of his Son, for forgiveness. "Facts are useful," Elder Neal A. Maxwell pointed out; "everlasting truths are critical. So much of real education consists of acquiring perspective about everlasting truths so that we can then manage, successfully, the transitory factual things, for tactical choices do crowd in upon us hour by hour. Knowing the facts about a bus schedule, for instance, is helpful, but such facts are clearly not the emancipating truths Jesus spoke of as being necessary to experience real freedom."[2]

Further, some things are relative; their composition or our perspective on them may change with new discoveries or new directions. Social trends or fads or novel world views may reconstitute such "truths." Other things are absolute: they are forever fixed, immutable, unchangeable. Their innate truthfulness is not determined by popularity or consensus. Disciples come to know which truths are relative and which are absolute.

113

"God, our Heavenly Father—Elohim—lives," stated President Spencer W. Kimball. "That is an absolute truth. All four billion of the children of men on earth might be ignorant of him and his attributes and his powers, but he still lives.

"All the people on the earth might deny him and disbelieve, but he lives in spite of them. They may have their own opinions, but he still lives, and his form, powers, and attributes do not change according to men's opinions. In short, opinion alone has no power in the matter of an absolute truth. . . .

"The watchmaker in Switzerland, with materials at hand, made the watch that was found in the sand of a California desert. The people who found the watch had never been to Switzerland, nor seen the watchmaker, nor seen the watch made. The watchmaker still existed, no matter the extent of their ignorance or experience. If the watch had a tongue, it might even lie and say, 'There is no watchmaker.' That would not alter the truth.

"If men are really humble, they will realize that they *discover*, but do not *create* truth."[3]

In an unusual directive given to the School of the Prophets, the Lord said: "And as all have not faith, seek ye diligently and teach one another words of wisdom; yea, seek ye out of the best books words of wisdom; *seek learning, even by study and also by faith*" (D&C 88:118; emphasis added). Most of us are familiar with learning by study. It is what we are taught to do from childhood. It consists of attuning the intellectual faculties, focusing upon the subject before us, and grasping the matters to be learned. It is a cognitive, rational process. But what of knowledge by faith? How do we acquire truth by faith? In one sense, we have already addressed this issue: there are some truths which only the faithful will come to understand. In a related way, we learn by faith when we do the will of the Lord, seeking for the ratifying and confirming influence of the Spirit, when we follow the Savior's formula of "do—then know" (John 7:16–17; compare Ether 12:6). We gain a witness of the Word of Wisdom or the law of tithing as we observe these laws, as we keep

114

them. We come to know of the truthfulness of the Book of Mormon as we read and ponder and then pray over the doctrines and principles and precepts contained therein. Do—then know. In this manner we exercise faith—we hope for what is unseen but true (Alma 32:21)—and then come to know.

To learn by faith is to learn by revelation, to acquire insight by the Holy Spirit of God speaking directly to our souls. President Marion G. Romney said: "Such truth is not to be had through man's ordinary learning processes. His sensory powers are calculated and adapted to deal only with the things of this telestial earth. Without revelation, man's intellect is wholly inadequate for the discovery of the ultimate truth with which the gospel deals."[4] One of the most profound statements ever made on this phenomenon of acquiring truth, or knowledge, by faith was made by President Harold B. Lee. "The acquiring of knowledge by Faith," he taught, "is no easy road to learning. It will demand continuous effort and continual striving by faith. In short, learning by faith is no task for a lazy man. Someone has said, in effect, that 'such a process requires the bending of the whole soul, the calling up from the depths of the human mind and linking the person with God. The right connection must be formed; then only comes knowledge by faith, a kind of knowledge that goes beyond secular learning, that reaches into the realms of the unknown and makes those who follow that course great in the sight of the Lord.' "[5]

To some degree education in general frees us from ignorance and from the bondage and servitude of our own situation or plight. But this does not seem to be the kind of truth to which our Savior had reference; he spoke of saving truths. In fact, the truths that are of greatest eternal worth may not be taught by man. The Apostle John taught that because of the unction, the anointing of the Holy Ghost, which the members of the Church had received, they needed not that any man teach them certain things (see 1 Jn. 2:27). Here, as in all things, the Lord Jesus Christ is the pattern for all who seek the path of discipleship. In speaking of the time in our Lord's life between the ages of twelve and

115

thirty, Matthew wrote: "And it came to pass that Jesus grew up with his brethren, and waxed strong, and waited upon the Lord for the time of his ministry to come. And he served under his father [presumably, Joseph], and *he spake not as other men, neither could he be taught; for he needed not that any man should teach him.* And after many years, the hour of his ministry drew nigh" (JST, Matt. 3:24–26; emphasis added). How wondrous it is that "by the power of the Holy Ghost ye may know the truth of all things" (Moro. 10:5).

There is an even deeper and more profound reality associated with the Lord's statement that we shall know the truth and the truth shall make us free. As we continue in his word, as we move forward in unsensational but steadfast fashion, as we come to live by every word of God, as we seek after and acquire the gifts and fruit of the Spirit, we come to know him who is the Truth: we come to know the Lord. We can come to know about the Lord by study. We come to know the Lord only by study in combination with faith. We know the Lord as we serve him and keep his commandments (see Mosiah 5:12–13; 1 Jn. 2:3–4). Jesus said: "I am the way, *the truth,* and the life: no man cometh unto the Father, but by me" (John 14:6; emphasis added). It is not just that the Son of God brought light into a darkened and fallen world; he *is* the Light (3 Ne. 11:11). It is not just that our Savior showed us the way; he *is* the Way (John 14:6). It is not just that Christ made the resurrection available; he *is* the resurrection (John 11:25). And it is not just that Jesus of Nazareth restored the truth and taught the truth; he *is* the Truth. Disciples who learn from and lean on and lead others to their Master come in time to know their Master. They gain "the mind of Christ" (1 Cor. 2:16). They are thus freed, liberated from the fetters of falsehood, the prison of a limited perspective, and the distorting lens of a fallen nature. Joseph Smith observed:

"We consider that God has created man with a mind capable of instruction, and a faculty which may be enlarged in proportion to the heed and diligence given to the light communicated from heaven to the intellect; and that the nearer man approaches

116

perfection, the clearer are his views, and the greater his enjoyments, till he has overcome the evils of his life and lost every desire for sin; and like the ancients, arrives at that point of faith where he is wrapped in the power and glory of his Maker and is caught up to dwell with Him."[6]

Disciples of Christ soon learn that acquiring the attributes of godliness entails far more than learning some facts. We do not practice the religion of Jesus Christ by study, intellectual preparation, and theological inquiry and discovery alone. Religion is a thing of the heart as well. "True religion," Elder Bruce R. McConkie once stated, deals with spiritual things.

"We do not come to a knowledge of God and his laws through intellectuality, or by research, or by reason. They are important enough in their sphere, but when contrasted with spiritual endowments, they are of but slight and passing worth. From an eternal perspective, what each of us needs is a Ph.D. in faith and righteousness. The things that will profit us everlastingly are not the power to reason, but the ability to receive revelation; not the truths learned by study, but the knowledge gained by faith; not what we know about the things of the world, but our knowledge of God and his laws.

In sum, "Religion comes from God by revelation and deals with spiritual things; and unless and until a man has received revelation, he has not received religion, and he is not on the path leading to salvation in our Father's kingdom."[7] It is vital that we know the truth. There is no salvation in falsehood, even in sincere falsehood. Christ is the Truth. As we grow in light and truth we grow unto him. We thereby become his.

NOTES

1. "The Spirit of Truth," in "To Be Learned Is Good If . . . ," ed. Robert L. Millet (Salt Lake City: Bookcraft, 1987), p. 231.

2. From a baccalaureate address delivered at Ricks College, 25 Apr. 1978.

3. "Absolute Truth," 1977 BYU Devotional Speeches of the Year, 6 Sept. 1977 (Provo, Utah: Brigham Young University Press, 1978), p. 138.

4. Look to God and Live (Salt Lake City: Deseret Book Co., 1971), p. 65.

5. *BYU Speeches of the Year*, 11 Sept. 1973 (Provo, Utah: Brigham Young University Press, 1973), p. 91.

6. *Teachings of the Prophet Joseph Smith*, sel. Joseph Fielding Smith (Salt Lake City: Deseret Book Co., 1976), p. 51.

7. In Conference Report, Apr. 1971, pp. 99, 101.

Chapter 21

YE SHALL HAVE ETERNAL LIFE

Following baptism by water, disciples are awarded the greatest gift given to mortals—the gift of the Holy Ghost. This sacred endowment is given to direct, tutor, comfort, cleanse, and purify us, to lead us along the path of life and keep us within a whisper of the Gods. The Holy Ghost expands the mind and opens the eyes so that followers of Christ may begin to see and feel things foreign to the spiritually uninitiated. As true disciples navigating the strait and narrow path, we face the tests and challenges of life and prove through deed and dedication an absolute willingness to serve God at all hazards. Thus by faithfulness we ultimately qualify for the greatest gift in eternity—exaltation, or eternal life.

We do not travel far before we realize that we cannot stay on the path or arrive at the desired end by ourselves. We must have help. That help is what the scriptures designate as *grace,* the freely given, enabling power to do what we could never do unaided. The fall of Adam was a universal fall; it affected humankind and all other forms of life. An infinite power was thereby required to effect the redemption of man and earth. An infinite power required an infinite Being. And so it was that Jesus, the son of Mary and the Son of God, demonstrated the greatest act of love and mercy in time or eternity. The atoning sacrifice ransomed us from physical death through the resurrection and also made eternal life—God's life, the glory of the celestial kingdom, the continuation of the family unit (D&C 88:4;

119

132:19)—a possibility for those who come unto Christ and partake of the cleansing powers of his blood.

The gospel covenant consists of a two-way promise between us and our Redeemer. First, Christ promises on his part that he will justify us, pronounce us clean, innocent, free from sin and stain. As disciples, we promise that we will accept the ransoming powers of Christ, repent of our sins, trust in the Lord, and seek thereafter to live the life of one called out of the world. As disciples, we agree to perform certain works that evidence our faith, which signify by deed our commitment to the gospel covenant. We agree to receive the ordinances of salvation, keep our thoughts, actions, and speech pure and within the prescribed bounds of morality and decency, and extend ourselves in acts of Christian service to our fellow beings. And yet the scriptures affirm repeatedly the solemn truth that our works alone cannot save us, cannot lead to life eternal. They are necessary but insufficient. In short, eternal life is not, in the purest sense, something which may be *earned*. It is the greatest of all the gifts of God (see D&C 6:13; 14:7), something which we *inherit* from an all-wise and all-loving God. As disciples of Christ we seek to please our Lord and Master by doing all that we can. But all that we can is not enough, and we know it. Our reliance is thus not in the arm of flesh, not even in our own arm. Our trust and reliance are wholly in the Savior. It is by the merits and mercy and grace of the Holy Messiah—his works—that we are saved, after all we can do (see 2 Ne. 2:3, 8; 25:23; 31:19; Alma 22:14; Moro. 6:4; D&C 45:3–5). Disciples pray fervently to know their own limits, to know when they have done all that can humanly be done; then the follower turns to the Leader and supplicates Him, seeking earnestly the supplementary strength and power to accomplish the task at hand.

And what is the spiritual barometer? How do disciples know if they are on course? How may they sense that their lives and labors will eventually be acceptable to Him who is perfect? We learn in time that we need not proceed toward the goal of exaltation in the dark; we need not wait and wonder and worry;

rather, "he who doeth the works of righteousness shall receive his reward, even peace in this world, and eternal life in the world to come." (D&C 59:23.) Peace here points toward the ultimate peace hereafter. Peace in this world portends the peace of eternal glory in the next world. Peace, the quiet but certain signal of divine acceptance, can be a daily indicator that the heavens are pleased and that we are on course. When the Lord speaks peace to our minds, it matters precious little what myopic mortals may think. When we feel such peace, we might well ask, as Christ did: "What greater witness can you have than from God?" (D&C 6:23.)

Isaiah taught almost thirty centuries ago: "And the work of righteousness shall be peace; and the effect of righteousness quietness and assurance for ever" (Isa. 32:17). Those in this life who conduct themselves with fidelity and devotion to God and his laws shall eventually know the peace "which passeth all understanding" (Philip. 4:7), the calming but powerful assurance that they have successfully met the challenges of mortality. These are they who as disciples of the Christ have lived by every word of God. They have made their callings and elections sure.[1] For them the day of judgment has been advanced, and the blessings associated with exaltation in the celestial kingdom are assured. Though it is true, as President Marion G. Romney observed, that "the fulness of eternal life is not attainable in mortality, . . . the peace which is its harbinger and which comes as a result of making one's calling and election sure is attainable in this life."[2]

Latter-day Saints who have received the ordinances of salvation—including the blessings of the temple endowment and eternal marriage—may thus press forward as true disciples in the work of the Lord and with quiet dignity and patient maturity seek to be worthy of gaining the certain assurance of salvation before the end of their mortal lives. But should we not formally receive the more sure word of prophecy—the knowledge that we are sealed to eternal life (D&C 131:5–6)—in this life, we have the scriptural promise that faithfully enduring to the end, keeping the commandments and covenants to the end of our lives, eventuates in the promise of eternal life, whether that promise be received here or hereafter. "But blessed are they who are faithful and endure, *whether in life or in death, for they shall inherit eternal life*" (D&C 50:5; emphasis added). In other words, as Elder Bruce R. McConkie explained, "If we die in the faith, that is the same thing as saying that our calling and election has been made sure and that we will go on to eternal reward hereafter."[3]

These blessings are at the end of the path Nephi and Lehi saw in vision, a path not far removed from filthy waters, and certainly within earshot of the beckoning calls of those who have taken up lodging in the great and spacious building. That path leads through mists of darkness, divers temptations and allurements of the devil. But at the end of the path, for those who have held tenaciously and reverently to the rod of iron and who have maintained an eye of faith, is the fruit of the tree of life. "If ye will nourish the word," Alma said to the Zoramites, "yea, nourish the tree as it beginneth to grow, by your faith with great diligence, and with patience, looking forward to the fruit thereof, it shall take root; and behold it shall be a tree springing up unto everlasting life. And . . . by and by ye shall pluck the fruit thereof, which is most precious, which is sweet above all that is sweet, and which is white above all that is white, yea, and pure above all that is pure; and ye shall feast upon this fruit even until ye are filled, that ye hunger not, neither shall ye thirst" (Alma 32:41–42). King Benjamin spoke in the same vein of the great consummation to our discipleship which comes as we remain true and faithful to every trust. "Therefore, I would that ye should be steadfast and immovable, always abounding in good works, that Christ, the Lord God Omnipotent, may seal you his, that you may be brought to heaven, that ye may have everlasting salvation and eternal life, through the wisdom, and power, and justice, and mercy of him who created all things, in heaven and in earth, who is God above all" (Mosiah 5:15).

We are becoming here what we will be hereafter. That is to say, discipleship is the training camp for Godhood. By living the gospel in this life, we are quickened by a portion of that celestial glory which shall be bestowed in fulness in the resurrection (D&C 88:29). We are in preparation now for greater things, but we must be equipped and our souls adapted for such a transformation. We cannot be restored from negligence and indifference to glory and honor. In the words of President Lorenzo Snow, we shall find that "in the morning of the resurrection we will possess those acquisitions only which we acquired in this world! Godliness cannot be conferred but must be acquired."[4]

Our Savior beckons, "Come, follow me." The road is long, and the costs are great. But if we desire to go where he is, we must be willing to go where he has been. Those who have tasted of the sweet fruit of the Spirit have been given a foretaste of that which is to be, and they eagerly lay down their all in the cause of truth. They are willing to go and say and be all that their beloved Master would desire of them. The Prophet Joseph Smith wrote to his wife Emma: "I will try to be contented with my lot, knowing that God is my friend; in him I shall find comfort. I have given my life into his hands. I am prepared to go at his call. I desire to be with Christ. I count not my life dear to me, only to do his will."[5] Such is the duty and disposition of the disciple. Temporary trials fade into insignificance, however, when we ponder upon the peace and happiness now available, as well as the eternal glories that follow faithful service. "Ye cannot behold with your natural eyes, for the present time, the design of your God concerning those things which shall come hereafter, and the glory which shall follow after much tribulation. For after much tribulation come the blessings" (D&C 58:3–4). Such is the reward and the prize of the disciple. And indeed, it is worth any cost that must be paid along the way.

NOTES

1. See *Teachings of the Prophet Joseph Smith,* sel. Joseph Fielding Smith (Salt Lake City: Deseret Book Co., 1976), pp. 149–51, 298, 300, 305.

2. In Conference Report, Oct. 1965, p. 20.

3. From an address at funeral service for Elder S. Dilworth Young, 13 July 1981, typescript, p. 5.

4. *Millennial Star,* 13:362.

5. In *The Personal Writings of Joseph Smith,* ed. Dean C. Jessee (Salt Lake City: Deseret Book Co., 1984), p. 239; punctuation standardized.

Index

125

127